NORTH EAST FOLK

By the same author

I Bought a Windmill

NORTH EAST FOLK

From Cottage to Castle

Elizabeth Adair

Paul Harris Publishing

Edinburgh

First published 1982 by
Paul Harris Publishing
40 York Place
Edinburgh

ISBN 0 86228 031 1

Typeset in Scotland by John G Eccles, Printers Ltd, Inverness
Printed and bound by William Collins Sons & Co. Ltd.

Contents

Illustrations

Scotland (Grampian Region), Douglas McDonald head gardener at Crathes
Castle, Anne Cocker, Anne Murray and Jenny Hillson.
24. The beautiful Silver Jubilee Rose.

Cocky Hunter
25. The exterior of Cocky Hunter's Store in Castle Terrace in 1955.
26. Alex Hunter — Cocky Hunter the Second.
27. Bill Hunter and his wife cutting the cake at their Gold Wedding in 1978.

Mary McMurtrie
28. Balbithan House, Kintore.
29. The Garden at Balbithan.
30. Mary McMurtrie having tea in the garden.

Jessie Kesson
31. Jessie Kesson (left) with the author at the BBC in 1950.

George Barron
32. George Barron (right) with two other judges Tom Brayshaw and Mrs Helen
    Chalmers at the Britain in Bloom Competition looking at Bill Laing's
    garden in Campsie Place, Aberdeen.
33. The 17th Century Great Garden of Pitmedden where George Barron was
    head gardener until 1978.

People who have Gardens
34. James Hird in his Council House Garden at Summerhill.
35. A corner of James Hird's garden.
36. Peter Kaminskas, the gardener, at Bellenden, Milltimber.

Bessie Brown
37. Bessie Brown, sitting in her garden at Heatherdale Cottage near Banchory.

Walter Leiper
38. Walter Leiper, the lapidarist, at his grinding machine in Garlogie School.
39. The old school and school-house where Walter Leiper has his gem-stone
    cutting business.

Harold Esslemont
40. Harold Esslemont photographing Alpine plants in the Swiss Mountains.

H. Adair Nelson
41. My father, H. Adair Nelson, in the garden at 65 Osborne Place in 1922
    before setting out for the theatre in the evening.
42. Family group of the Adair Nelsons taken in 1921 — self, Peggy, Hal, my
    mother and Bill.
43. The interior of His Majesty's Theatre in 1957, the 'Watteau' curtain
    already replaced by the red velvet drapes.
44. The exterior of His Majesty's Theatre, Aberdeen taken in 1906 the year the
    theatre opened. Schoolhill Railway Station and Black's Buildings on the
    right (since demolished).
45. Les Fêtes Venitiennes by Watteau on which was based the painting on the
    theatre curtain called The Minuet.

Preface

THE theme of this book is that of personal endeavour of North East folk past and present whether they live in cottage or castle. Some of the folk are no longer with us but all leave their mark in different spheres — the traditional farmers, soldiers, sheep breeders, gardeners, craftsmen, writers. They reflect a more leisurely way of life and I for one regret its passing.

E.A.   *Aboyne, Aberdeenshire*

*To my sister Peggy
who shared my memories*

Chapter 1

George Conn, Private No. 3932
1st Company 79th Cameron Highlanders

> As I gaed doon tae Turra Market,
> Turra Market for tae fee,
> I fell in wi' a wealthy fairmer
> Frae the barnyards o' Delgatie.
>
> I can drink and no' be drunk,
> I can fecht and no' be slain,
> I can coort anither man's lass
> And aye be welcome tae my ain.

SO runs the famous bothy ballad of the farming area of Delgatie near Turriff in Aberdeenshire. The barnyards lie not far from Delgatie Castle, the imposing 15th century five storied stronghold of the great family of Hay, Earls of Erroll, High Constables of Scotland.

A young woman named Lillias Conn, daughter of William Conn, grieve to the Laird of Mountblairy near Banff, lived a hundred and thirty years ago at Delgatie Castle where her aunt Betsy was housekeeper, working in the ancient, wide-fireplaced, vaulted kitchen in the basement. Lillias herself was lady's maid at the castle.

For many years she kept as her dearest possession at the back of a little mahogany display case a bundle of letters written to her between 1854 and 1855 by her soldier brother George Conn, Private No. 3932 in the 79th Cameron Highlanders serving in the Crimea. After her death in 1900 the letters passed from one member of her family to another until they were shown to me in 1955 by two brothers, grandsons of Lillias Conn — John and William Weir.

I have these letters from the Crimea on the table in front of

me now. The envelopes are very small with three one penny
Victorian stamps on them, addressed via Marseilles. The writing,
ink now faded to brown, is copperplate — sign of young George's
education at the Mountblairy Estate School. The style is the
simple speech of the country loon. With the co-operation of the
two brothers I presented readings from the letters at the B.B.C. in
Aberdeen in 1955. I felt the letters should also appear in print.

Early in 1854 the British Government officially announced its
involvement in the War in the Balkans. George, like many others,
was only seventeen when he volunteered in November of that
year. A severe early winter had struck Aberdeenshire when the
snow lay on the ground for months on end and work in the rural
areas was hard to find. The Army was offering generous bounties
to recruits. The 79th Cameron Highlanders Depot was at Aberdeen Barracks behind the Castlegate and every day twenty or
thirty recruits from all parts of Scotland arrived in Aberdeen. A
hundred recruits at a time were drilled amidst the towering piles of
snow in the Barracks Square. Then after only six or eight weeks
training they were shipped abroad to the Crimea to join the
regiment which along with the 42nd and 93rd composed the
Highland Brigade under Sir Colin Campbell, afterwards the great
Lord Clyde of the Indian Mutiny.

By the time the letters begin the accounts of the battles of Alma,
Balaclava and Inkerman were well-known at home. The storm at
Balaclava on November 13 1854 had wrecked the ships with the
provisions and winter clothing for the soldiers and they were ill
equipped to cope with the extremes of the Crimean climate. But
the first carefree letters were written from Aberdeen Barracks.

January 14th 1855

Dear Sister,
    I write you this few lines to let you know that I reached Aberdeen safe
on Wednesday night and I learned when I came back here that I was not
going away with the Draft on Monday as there is nine of the fellows that
was absent come back and so I have not to go now. You will tell Betsy
that I have lost the receipt for Galetine that I was to send to her but I will
get it again as it was some of the rest in the room that has taken it away
but I shall soon get it again. The men going with the draft is all confined
to barracks at half past nine on Monday morning. They are all in very
good spirits just now and wishing they were away.
    I promised to send Betsy a piece of poetry written by the man you saw
who was reduced in the cells when you saw him. It is called Farewell as

he is leaving Scotland. I shall conclude at this time and remain your,
loving brother,
GEORGE CONN.
P.S. Write soon.

He writes next from Balaclava on June 6 1855. The long gap
between January 14th and the 25th of May when his company
landed is unbridgeable. But reports were already reaching Britain
of the conditions of squalor and disease the soldiers were forced to
suffer — reports mainly from the pen of the eminent *Times*
correspondent William Howard Russell who had been sent out to
the Balkans on behalf of his newspaper. His reports coincided
with the arrival of Florence Nightingale in Scutari dedicated to
provide medical care for the troops. He wrote:

"It is now pouring rain the skies black as ink — the wind is
howling over the staggering tents — the trenches are turned into
dykes — in the tents the water is sometimes a foot deep. Our men
have not either warm or waterproof clothing — they are out for
twelve hours at a time in the trenches — they are plunged into the
miseries of a winter campaign — and not a soul seems to care for
their comfort or even for their lives."

This was the period supposed to consist of "nice little evening
parties" when the enemy's outposts had to be seized during the
long siege before the storming of Sebastopol.

George Conn gives his own description of the conditions.

79th Highlanders
Balaklava
June 6th, 1855.

Dear sister,

I am greatly astonished at you not writing sooner but I suppose the
letter has been lost or something for I have not got a letter from you
since I left Aberdeen. May I tell you now that I am in enemy's country.
I came in on the 25th of May and we was only about four hours landed
when we had to stand-to and very soon after there was about 40
thousand of the enemy come marching up but their errand was to
reconnoitre or see our position when we got the order to load and the
blood run cold through my veins and I felt a shiver come on me but
before I had the firelock loaded I felt I could advance bold enough. So
after standing for four hours under arms we was ordered to fall out and
go to sleep and it came on one of the terriblest nights of rain that ever
fell from the heavens but for all that we slept very soundly and I
happened to lie on a furrow and when I wakened the water was fast
covering me. I think that tried my feelings pretty well at the first but I
have not had the like of it again — I have not much time to tell you

about the country until I write again as our Company is ordered to do
duty before Sebastopol. So next time I write I can give you a right
description of the Seige that is going on there. You will give my kind
love to Aunt Betsy and Grandmother and tell them I am in good health
and give my best wishes to George Malcolm and his family and tell him
this is a fine country for hares and patridges for the other night while
making sentry on the ridge of a hill they were flocking about me in
thousands and they came so near that I killed five of them with the butt
of my firelock and almost every foraging party brings home about a
dozen or so hares with them. This is a piece of an officer's kilt that was
killed yesterday and he was so well liked that every man requested a
piece of his kilt to keep or send home to their friends. His name was
Captain Henry Reid and his loss is greatly felt in the regiment for the
like of him will never fill his place. He was what the soldiers called the
79th's friend.

The piece of kilt has been lost unfortunately, perhaps never
received at Delgatie.

The next of these letters, which only took three or four weeks to
reach Turriff, has a lot to say about trench warfare and even more
about the high prices they paid for everything. The men received a
minimum of 1/- per day (5 new pence) plus 1d. per day (½ a new
penny) beer money. From this total was deducted the cost of
rations and regimental stoppages, leaving them with 2d. a day.
Greektown which he mentions is to the east of Balaclava and a
day's shopping meant a tramp of sixteen miles and the spending of
two months' pay.

HEIGHTS BEFORE SEBASTOPOL
July 31st 1855.
Dear Sister,
      I received your letter of the 29th of June and I was glad to hear by it
that you are all in good health as this few lines leaves me enjoying part of
the same pleasure. We are always under fire of the enemy and there is
no hope of being any other way only we believe there is another grand
attack on the 21st of August and there is four companies of the 79th,
400 of the 42nd and 400 of the 93rd all for the storming party or forlorn
hope so I doubt some of us will stand a bad chance of ever returning to
Scotland again. I had a very narrow escape on the 14th. At about eleven
o' clock they made a determined sortie and our Regiment was lying in
the advanced trench; the night was very dark and wet and our firelocks
having got damp they would not go off, and we was thrown into a little
confusion but it was soon over for we just kept into the trench and every
Russian that tried to come to the parapet received about six bayonets in
his body at once. So one having tumbled into the trench after being
wounded I tried to pop some of my powder down the nipple of my gun
to make her go off when the treacherous de'il fired his gun at me and the

ball passed through the neck of my greatcoat and just grazed the skin a little which astonished me a little for had it been another eighth of an inch nearer I would have been shot through the neck. That night we lost five killed and eight wounded all owing to our firelocks being damp. The whole of the soldiers here is beginning to fear the stopping another winter lying under canvas roofs and walls, and all volunteering to either lose the life or take the town and get into barracks. It is beginning to get very cold at night and a man lying in the trenches feels very chilly before the sunrise in the morning and then when morning comes in we take a sleep and when the sun gets so warm that you can't sleep but go away to look for some wood to boil your coffee for breakfast and a piece of a shovel to roast your pork on and then you commence cooking as quick as you can get a fire to burn. The only thing that vexes the men is the dearness of the new potatoes. They are 9d a pound, butter is 4/- a pound and cheese 3/6 and you will pay tenpence for half an ounce of tea. We just clear 2d a day here or 5/- a month which is very easy spent when you go to buy any necessaries of that kind. I went away the other day with two months pay — ten shillings — to a place called Greektown about 8 miles from our camp expecting to make a better market there. I bought a new shirt 6/6; a dozen of shirt buttons for 2/-; 2 needles for 6d and a hank of thread for 1/- so you may guess how things sell in this part of the world. I wish you to put your address on your letters as that is the way they would let you know if I was hurt or killed for our lives is not insured here nor we don't know the minute we may get the head knocked off. I shall add no more at this time. Give my kind love to aunt Betsy and all enquiring friends and I remain your affectionate Brother,
George Conn,
3932
1st Company 79th Highlanders
British Army in the Crimea.

Two more letters arrived in quick succession first to his sister passing lightly over the "bit of a squabble" which he then has some relish in describing to his uncle William Conn. Several times he refers to his General, Sir Colin Campbell, already famous for his achievements in the Crimea.

Camp before Sebastopol,
August 7th 1855.

Dear Sister,
    I received your kind and affectionate letter likewise one from Uncle the same day and I was happy to hear by them that you are all in good health as this is about to leave me enjoying part of the same good blessing thank God for it — I have very little news to tell you of, only just now and then having a bit of a fight while you quiet folks about Delgaty hears no musket balls or bomb shells flying about you ears the same as the bold fellows here do. I may mention the Highland Brigade

has volunteered to be the storming party or forlorn hope at the next attack on Sebastopol to be led by our old General Sir Colin Campbell and I may plainly say — that them that comes back will be lucky — to tell the work of the day come of it when it may. You will give my kind love to aunt Betsy. I shall add no more but remain your loving and affectionate brother,
George Conn.

Dear Uncle,
     Your affectionate letter I duly received . . . We are always having a bit of a squabble now and then with the Russians — on the night of the 4th of this we had a pretty severe struggle but we came off with the best of it — it was a very dark and rainy night and the sentries had not seen them advancing until they were on the top of them, and with the fright they retired from the advanced trench and his and the 93rd being in the rear trench there was a little confusion when we had to advance and we had to get on the best way we could through the broken ranks of the 34th and by this time there was upwards of two thousand of the enemy into the trench the 34th had left and us only five hundred strong, but by the good luck the 18th regiment of Royal Irish had come down on the other flank of the trench. When that became known to the Highlanders they with one shout or rather a yell they rushed upon the astonished Russians and the clatter of bayonet to bayonet became furious. The Russians wheeled about to retire but they soon found themselves between Highlanders and wild Irishmen which was the worst position they ever were in. We took 115 prisoners and we had to lie all night in the trench among 250 dead and wounded Russians and had to put about 20 of them into bunches to get a place to sit down in, not to be lying in the middle or on top of them. And when morning began to dawn the stripping commenced and everybody that had a clean shirt on was very soon made quit of it. I thought myself pretty well when I got three new cotton shirts off three of them. Through the day we dug a pit and pitched 189 of them into their grave there along with 6 of the 79th and eleven of the 93rd and we grumbled terribly to have the killing and burying of them both . . .
     I may mention that I have seen two of the old man Smith the weaver in Aberdeenshire's sons and there one of them is slightly wounded in the hand and he thinks he will be sent home and discharged. If you have any old Aberdeen or Banff Journals you might send them out. You have to put two stamps and address via Marseilles for we get no papers but our friends' and when one man in a company gets a paper everyone runs crying 'Give us a look after you'. I shall finish at this time remaining your loving and affectionate nephew,
George Conn.

Many of the exploits of the Scottish soldiers in the Crimea were commemorated in verse and song in the North East of Scotland, like the tale of the "Horsemen's wives" in the song "The Kilties in the Crimea" during the storming of Sebastopol.

Sir Colin waved his sword on high,
Then wi' a wild unearthly cry,
Up rushed the kilties to the foe,
And felled a man at every blow.
Ower horses, men, and guns they speeled,
And cleared the Russians frae the field,
While far and near was heard the cheer
Aboon the pibroch sounding clear.

The Russian General, when he saw
The Kilties chase his men awa'
Cried oot, "Does ony mortal ken
Whether they're wild beasts or men?"
Sir Colin cried, "Come here, my man,
And I will tell, for weel I can,
The kilted lads are just," he says
"Our horsemen's wives in Sunday claes."

The Russian horsemen charged them then,
Our horsemen's wives stood up like men,
And gied them sic a dose o' lead
That a' ran aff that werena dead.
But a' oor wives and woman folk
Wi' perfect joy are like to choke.
And mony a ane'll get a smack
When the gallant kilted lads come back.

But not all the gallant kilted lads came back.

Heights before Sebastopol,
14th August 1855.

Madam,
    I have to acquaint you with the sad tidings of the death of your Dear Brother. He was killed on the spot by the fragments of a shell bursting in one of the trenches yesterday forenoon. I feel it is my duty as a Comrade and a Dear Acquaintance, he being in the same tent and in the same Company with me since he joined the Regiment, to be the first to acquaint you. As a confidential friend of his he gave me your address some time ago in the event of anything happening, but believe me my dear Miss that little did either of us think that one of us was to be cut off so soon. But I hope the Lord will strengthen you and make you able to bear up against this sad affliction for I am well aware of the grief you will feel when you see the sad tidings of the death of your dear and only brother.

Your friend and wellwisher
DAVID HILL NICOLSON
CORPORAL NO. 1 COMPANY
79th HIGHLANDERS.

George Conn was under nineteen when he fell and didn't see the final bombardment of Sebastopol. The Crimea took a heavy toll of lives in the Cameron Highlanders. Corporal David Nicolson was a regular soldier of about thirty-four at the time with thirteen years service.

In his next letter he writes to William Conn, uncle of George, from Kamara and the line of heights to the west of Balaclava.

8th January 1856.

Dear Friend,

I am happy to inform you that we are much better off here this winter than what we were the last. Since Sebastopol is taken we have no trench duty which was the most hard and dangerous duty that we had to perform for you will remember that it was doing trench duty that George met with his untimely end. We had to lie flat on the ground. I have seen one shell killing and wounding six of our men all because we had not cover enough to protect us. I am enclosing in this letter the St. Andrew and number of the Regiment that George wore in his Glengarry on that eventful morning. I will be obliged to you to tell Miss Conn that they are the only things that I could send her in remembrance of her brother.

The St. Andrew is the cap badge worn not very different from the badge now worn by the Cameron Highlanders. The two relics, the badge and numeral 79, reached Delgatie safely and are in the possession of the family.

According to the 79th News the Battalion left the Crimea to return to Britain in July 1856. Nicolson wrote once more to William Conn from Dover.

Dear Sir,

The principle object of my writing to you at this time is to desire you to make enquiry about your deceased nephew's medal and clasp for Sebastopol — it will be a relict. It is nothing but what you are entitled to only for the asking and at the same time you must ask about the money that was drawn for the sale of his kit and also ask if he had any money in the Captain of the Company's hands as we were in the habit at that time not to draw our pay regular.

I pray the Lord may bless and prosper you and yours is the sincere wish of your wellwisher and friend,

David Hill Nicolson.

Over a year after George's death a letter from the War Department.

29th October 1856.

William Conn,

I am directed to transmit to you herewith a medal which has been

granted for the late George Conn's service as a soldier of the 79th
Regiment of Foot to be kept in commemoration of his gallant conduct
in the Crimean Campaign at Sebastopol.

These are the letters. They tell a simple story which has been
repeated before and since a thousand thousand times. Though
there exists no likeness of him, George Conn seems known to us
like the farmer's boy in the ballad The Barnyards o' Delgatie.

My cannle noo it is brunt oot.
My snotter's fairly on the wane,
Sae fare ye well, ye barnyards,
Ye'll never catch me here again!

Chapter 2

Royal Gardener

IT is a far cry from the misery of the war in the Crimea to the peace and solitude of Deeside, yet it was in the gardens of Birkhall on the estate of Balmoral that Florence Nightingale strolled one autumn day in 1856 with Queen Victoria and divulged her unprecedented plans for a desperately needed Army medical service. The then Secretary of State for war, Lord Panmure, arrived at Balmoral a few weeks later for his term of attendance, and the Queen commanded a meeting between him and Miss Nightingale. To win over Lord Panmure might have been a formidable task for the "Lady of the Lamp" but for the support and persuasiveness of the Sovereign and the Prince Consort. The proposal for the Royal Commission, which ultimately led to the establishment of the Royal Army Medical Corps, was developed and granted in the Deeside garden of Birkhall within sight of the birch clad Coyles of Muick. Perhaps they sat under the very lime tree on the lawn that shaded me, for this magnificent tree is almost 160 years old.

But where is the house of Birkhall? Unseen from the road, it lies to the west side of the River Muick, a mile or so from the pretty little bridge over the river at Bridgend Cottages, not far from the meeting of the waters of Muick and Dee. As you approach the private entrance drive on the South Deeside Road, what remains of Knock Castle looks down on the road and the woodland, home of roe deer and fawns. This ruinous tower-hour was the tragic scene of the annihilation of the entire family of Gordon of Knock in the late 16th century.

But this spring day I had happier thoughts than old Scottish feuds as I drove, past the sentry box, down the steep descent to the white harled residence of Her Majesty Queen Elizabeth the Queen Mother. Built in 1715 by Rachel Gordon, 10th Laird of Abergeldie and her husband Charles Gordon, it was a typical "Ha" house of the period, of two storeys with attic accommodation for servants. Over the original entrance, reached by a charming stone staircase with white painted handrails, is the inscription with date and initials.

17   C.G.   R.G.   15

About 130 years later Prince Albert bought the property from the Gordons intending it to become the Scottish home of his eldest son the Prince of Wales, afterwards Edward VII. Finding it too small the Prince sold it in 1885 to his mother Queen Victoria and it has remained part of the Balmoral Estate ever since.

In January 1957 a temporary annexe of corrugated iron was demolished and an extensive plan of restoration was carried out by the architect, A. Graham Henderson of Glasgow. Designed to blend with the original style of architecture of the house, two new wings were built and the whole roofed with the beautiful blue-grey slates from the neighbouring quarry Meall Dubh (The Black Hill).

And so to the garden which was originally planned and laid out at the turn of the century. The Queen Mother since taking occupation has made a point of retaining the most attractive features. She calls it "a delicious garden" and indeed it is, reflecting her deep love of flowers. The Head Gardener in charge, James Kerr, met me at the imposing "porte cochère", Victorian addition to the east side of the house, and we went through the most charming arched wrought iron gate bought by the Queen Mother at a recent Royal Highland Show. It was the prize-winning exhibit in the Blacksmith's Section. Delicately worked iron flowers and fruits of all seasons — roses, thistles, daffodils, apples, grapes and acorns are entwined through the lattice of the gateway. If you stand with your back to the gate you can glimpse between the openings among the copper beech, lime trees and firs the town of Ballater and the hills of Craigendarroch, Culblean and Morven.

Mr Kerr has been gardener at Birkhall for ten years. He came over from the farm at nearby Abergeldie Castle where, although he was a dairy farmer, he already had an extensive greenhouse. We crossed the lawn in front of the house and came to "The Eagle's Nest" — a summer house set high upon a hillock reached by shallow wooden steps cut into the bank at one time a mass of multi-coloured polyanthus but recently transformed into a rockery to display fine Alpine plants. From this viewpoint spreads a breath-taking panorama of lawns, terrace and formal garden dipping down to the clear waters of the River Muick rippling over

its smooth boulders. Following the contours of the river curves the
fruit and vegetable growing area, rich with French beans, peas and
cabbages and raspberries and strawberries and old cordon-trained
apple trees. And beyond — the meadows with red-brown Luing
cattle, reaching to the beech, birch and larch trees of Craig Vallich.

In the flower beds around the house and under all the windows
were pink "Clara Butt" tulips, interspersed with blue myosotis
and the pale violet clematis called "Mrs Cholmondely", sending
its first tendrils up the wall.

Later in the year in time for the Queen Mother's summer visit
the tulips will be replaced by her own choice of flowers in the
pastel shades she loves — creamy antirrhinums, blue campanulas,
purple alyssum, mauve sweet peas and peach and tangerine
nemesia. In front of the french window opening from the drawing-room is a small paved patio where Her Majesty and her guests
have afternoon tea on sunshiny days. A cypress hedge, twenty feet
high, forms a wind-break to the east running from the corner of
the house to the terrace and converting the lawn into a sun-trap.

The scent of the newly mown grass — two days work for two
gardeners — reminded me that in earlier times there were six
gardeners here. Then a pony was employed to pull the lawn
mowers, a boy leading the pony and a man sitting on the mower.
The pony wore special leather boots to prevent damage to the
lawn.

The spikes of the purple red Lythrum were already fringing the
summit of the terrace wall, soon to become an uninterrupted band
of colour.

A six foot wide border of coral pink "Windsor" phlox, its colour
enhanced by the silver-leaved foliage plant "Silver Dust", will line
the steep stairway leading from the terrace to the ornamental
topiared yew at the far end of the garden. The Queen Mother
suggested that flower beds in the shape of the initials E.R. should
be cut in the banks of grass sloping away from the terrace. The
beds will be filled with the striking combination of deep blue
lobelia and orange French marigolds.

By August the floribunda roses will be in full flower. Most
suitable for the soil and weather of Upper Deeside are the Royal
Favourites — "Honeymoon" the vigorous canary yellow rosette-
shaped blooms; Europeana a brilliant blood red with copper
leaves; "Glen Fiddich", golden amber with foliage of bronze; and
the superlative "Silver Jubilee" merging through pink, peach,

apricot and cream and named by permission of Her Majesty the
Queen in 1977, her Silver Jubilee Year. Careful watch must be
kept when the roses are coming into bud because in one night an
intruding roe-deer might invade and nip all the succulent shoots.
As the Queen Mother said "They're not very good gardeners, are
they!"

She has of course her favourite walks through the policies with
her two corgis, Geordie and Blackie. One walk leads to the steel
bridge which sways ever so slightly over the tumbling Muick as
you tread gingerly across it. Its appearance of fragility belies its
strength. Again she enjoys walking on the little island of rough
weeds and primroses which divides the river Muick in two.
Snowberry bushes have been planted on the island to prevent the
fast water washing away the soil from this sanctuary for birds.

On leaving the garden I found the traffic held up as I rejoined
the main road. A line of cars was waiting for a hen pheasant
followed by an Indian file of a dozen day-old chicks to cross to the
other side. A moment later they were succeeded by a mother stoat
with her family of young ones, so small they looked like furry
caterpillars.

Florence Nightingale must indeed have found peace at Birkhall
after the turmoil and tragedy of the Crimea.

Chapter 3

Jock and Mary Esson
of Wester Micras

AFTER one of the worst and longest and coldest winters I
remember, the grass was lush again, and the roads of Royal
Deeside were lined with golden broom, snowy wild geans and
white hawthorn and the rowan trees were heavy with pale green
blossom.

Barely two miles short of the village of Crathie, on the North
Deeside Road before you get to the Royal Family's Scottish homes
of Balmoral and Birkhall and just past the historic Castle of
Abergeldie, a steep turning on the right takes you up to Wester
Micras, a small farm on the Invercauld Estate. Other farms on the
land of Captain A.C. Farquharson, 16th Laird of Invercauld,
above and below Ballater are run by the staff of the Laird, but
Wester Micras is tenanted. The tenant farmer is Jock Esson who,
at the age of 80, still works the farm in company with his wife
Mary.

It was a lovely day when I called and we sat on the rough grass
with their son Ian, who lives with them and is an agricultural
contractor. The farm is set upon a hill overlooking to the south the
magnificent view of the curving River Dee where the sun was
striking silver patterns aslant the water. Through the fir trees to
the west, we could glimpse the red spire of Crathie Kirk where the
Queen Mother and other members of the Royal Family worship
when they are in residence on Deeside. In the distance the summit
of dark Lochnagar, its corries still patched with snow. Behind us
the typical sturdy little Scottish farmhouse with two rooms below
and two dormered windows above. When the Essons came to the
farm, thirty-one years ago, a bathroom was added and the steading
which was "a' tumelled in" was repaired. Above the house and to
the north they have broken the land and re-seeded atop of the hill,
where there are still scattered remains of many old deserted crofts.
In front of the house grows a young crab apple tree, the fruit "a

bittie bitter, but guid for jelly." The fields for their cattle and
sheep run down to the main road where the summer traffic speeds
on towards Braemar.

I asked Mrs Esson if she ever dropped her work to stand and
stare at this most picturesque scene, but she said she'd no time —
"never a clear day to myself".

Before Jock Esson took over Wester Micras, he was fee'd for
many years as a sheperd at Auchtavan, Aberarder. One of the "old
school", he favours traditional methods of farming. None of the
modern intensive methods for him. The 58 acres of arable land are
sufficient for his crops of oats, turnips and hay, while the 1,000
acres of hill carry his beasts all summer and winter. He has
seventeen cows, all crosses — black and blue mixture — with
Hereford cross calves.

When the services of a bull are required, a Hereford bull is hired
from Hillock of Keig, near Alford. One cow is reserved as the
house cow — that is she alone supplies the house with milk. Her
calf therefore is hand-fed from a pail, otherwise it would take all its
mother's milk. This "cogged calfie" is always of high quality.
Seven or eight years ago Jock Esson took the 5 month old calf to
the Aboyne Mart. Before the sale he was asked by a dealer what he
expected. "A damn lot mair than the like o' you would gi'e me," he
joked. It topped the sale that year at £228 for a Friesian cross steer!

I asked him how the animals had survived this last appalling
winter when the snow had lain for three months. He answered in
his rich couthy accent — "A devilish harsh winter. An afa'
deepness o' sna' — The coos looked as if they were made o' sna', so
white they were." But they all came through it. The struggle was
getting out to them every day at the top of the park to hand-feed
them, putting in the troughs the hay and sugar-beet and cattle cobs
for the cows, and sugar-beet, corn and ewe-pencils for the black-
face sheep. "My strong wife did the biggest half, she's a bit
younger than me. We never lost sheep or cattle ower the heids o'
the sna'." Despite the hard weather their lambing was successful.
Today, they have 145 ewes and 200 lambs.

He told me stories of days past. As a young man in the late
1920's, he was fee'd as a shepherd and herded the sheep for his
boss at a croft where he bothied. It was called Auchtavan and it lies
at the back of Inver Hotel.

He "traivelled" five hundred 5-month-old grey-face lambs from
Auchtavan to Aberdeen Belmont Mart. The journey on foot took

seven days, down by Crathie, through the Pass of Ballater, straight
on to Tarland, then Corse, the Crossroads Hotel, the steep hill of
Clash, Tornaveen, Midmar, then right on to Echt, Garlogie
thence to Belmont Mart. Every night the sheep were put into a
fenced field, and he and his companion shepherds were accommo-
dated in the house. But, "nothing special — nae much thought of
— shepherds!" At the mart the sheep fetched 16/- a head.

The cottage of Auchtavan is now the property of the Queen
Mother, a Royal residence in miniature. Restored and modernised
with a fenced off lawn in front it provides a delightful picnic spot
for the Queen Mother with a breath-taking view of the Cairngorms.

The Queen, her father and grandfather in turn used to shoot
above the farm on Micras Moor. Accompanied by her private
detective the Queen still comes with other members of the Royal
Family through the parks on the way to pheasant and partridge
shooting. Jock remembered one day when the Duchess of Kent
was almost run down by the binder in the narrow "roadie" cut
along the boundary of the field. He said "A nice body. She turned
roon' at the edge of the corn, smiled and said 'God Bless You'."

Mrs Esson looks after the hens — 89 brown Leghorns and a few
pullets. They range freely and happily about the farm and she has
strong views about the battery system. "A terrible thing. Hens in
cages. Flesh is nae the same as free hens. Too artificial the life and
feed. People say free range are too much work but for the sake of
the beast I say no. Leave them to their freedom. Here they have
their natural picks. They pick blades o' green grass, wee steenies
aff the road and fleas and beasties. Battery hens never see this."

After the needs of the house are satisfied, the large brown eggs
are sold locally to boarding houses and "bed and breakfasts".
Although it can be tricky sometimes gathering the eggs! One, "a
devil o' a hen" laid an egg on the landing at the top of the stair. The
nests in the hen house weren't good enough for her apparently, for
now she's trying to make a nest in the gas cooker! Then she got up
on the tractor to lay on the seat and the farmer sat right on top of an
egg.

The fields were strewn with daisies, the sun was so hot, the nine
pure bred white Aylesbury ducks, fostered by a brown hen, were
paddling happily in the stream. Indeed, battery hens never see
this!

As well as the hens, Mrs Esson tends the garden where in

abundance grow carrots, cabbages, tatties, onions, rasps and strawberries. She has just laid out an extra bit of garden ploughed from coarse grass by her son. Sheltered by gean trees to the west it will provide the house with vegetables all the year round. A wild honeysuckle hedge along one side has suddenly become luxuriant. Mrs Esson explained this by quoting a saying that if you work the garden beside it the honeysuckle will come on.

The day after my visit was to be sheep-shearing day. For the farmer's wife it meant five men to feed — dinner of soup, meat and pudding, at tea-time sandwiches and plenty to drink for sheep clipping is hot and thirsty work and a country high tea in the evening.

Jock says that now at his age he just does the odd jobs — bringing in the cattle and sheep, sawing wood and scything "thristles". But from what I could see, in an energy crisis they would be more than self-sufficient with birch logs, peat and kindling, chickens, eggs, milk, vegetables, fruit and the indomitable spirit of the traditional farmer. Jock's last words to me — "We've made money, lost money, but we're quite a' richt like. Canna afford to pay for labour. One thing — we're not in debt. We're both strong and well and happy."

Chapter 4

Farquharson of Invercauld and The Regalia

I mentioned that Wester Micras Farm, of which the tenant farmers were Jock and Mary Esson, lay on the Invercauld Estate. Invercauld House itself lies eight miles west of the little farm but only three miles short of Braemar, set high in the woodlands over unsurpassed views of the River Dee. In winter the red deer come down from the hills and wander freely in the parkland around the house. The entrance gates to the drive are almost opposite the beautiful four-arched military bridge — Invercauld Bridge — built over the river in 1753.

Captain Alwyne Compton Farquharson is 16th Laird of Invercauld and Chief of the Clan Farquharson since 1949. During the last war he served with the Royal Scots Greys in North Africa, Italy and France and was awarded the Military Cross. He is neighbouring landowner to the Queen and as a Vice Patron of the Braemar Royal Highland Society he greets her and members of the Royal Family on their arrival at the lovely tree encircled arena where every year in September the world famous Braemar Gathering is held. He takes full advantage of the sporting activities provided by his Highland estate. He is farmer, former County Councillor, collector of Scottish gem-stones, lover of works of art. Most highly prized is what is known as the Regalia of Invercauld. Strictly speaking regalia means "Insignia of Royalty used at Coronations" but in this instance the word "regalia" presents the emblems of a noble family — jewels and tartans, swords and skeandhus, dress and accoutrements, crests and coats of arms, family heirlooms of all kinds. I was happy to accept the opportunity accorded to me to view this splendour.

The day I drove along the North Deeside Road from Aberdeen was a grey, grey day. Soft rain, penetrating as only Deeside rain can be, slipped off the car roof. "A dreich day", said a passing gamekeeper. Picnickers this Whitsuntide sat disconsolately on folding chairs within reach of their car-boot, sipping hot soup. Bordering the entrance avenue to the mansion the larch trees, some of the first to be imported into Scotland in the 18th century, bent their graceful arms under the weight of their mist-laden needles, while groups of cattle stood close together, backs to the wind. And then the house itself, the Scottish baronial style at its best. Built of silver-grey granite it is dominated by a high central tower from which the wings radiate east, north and west. At one time the house consisted of several buildings, the oldest a low vaulted chamber with masonry from 5 to 7 feet thick, dating back to the reign of the Scots King James IV, or even the early part of the 15th century. Alterations and extensions in the 17th and 19th centuries linked together the smaller buildings to create the magnificent turretted castle we see today. Over the main doorway the arms of the Clan Farquharson were sculptured on stone at the time when additions were made to the house between 1674 and 1679.

Captain Farquharson welcomed me into the house and immediately the sombre mauves, yellows and browns of the chill day I had left behind changed into a glory of colours in the furnishings and furbishings. This impression reached its height when I arrived in the library and my host showed me a saddle-cloth draped over a screen, a translation into brilliant colours of the coat of arms I had previously seen in stone above the front door. Over a hundred years old, the background of the saddle-cloth is mustard yellow felt on which has been hand embroidered in wools the details of the coat of arms. The arms are divided quarterly. The 1st and 4th quarterings have a red lion rampant on a gold field, the 2nd and 3rd have a fir tree growing out of a mount, and on a red chief — i.e. the upper part of the field — is the Royal Banner of Scotland and on a canton a hand issuing from the left side holding a dagger point downwards. Above the shield is the crest, visor and helmet surmounted by a red demi-lion holding a sword "in the dexter paw proper hilted and pomelled or". Each symbol has of course a special significance — the twig of fir was worn in the bonnet as a distinguishing mark in time of battle; Finlay Mor, founder of the House of Farquharson of Invercauld, was one of the standard bearers of Mary Queen of Scots at the Battle of Pinkie where he fell in 1547, and thus the right to have the Royal flag in the coat of arms was granted; the dagger commemorated the slaying of the Red Cumine of Strathbogy. The supporters of the coat of arms are two wild cats indicative of the rugged country from which all Farquharsons come.

The Arms of Invercauld were matriculated about 270 years ago by the then Lyon King of Arms — ". . . which coat above blasoned I declare to be the said John Farquharson of Invercauld his coat and bearings. In testimony whereof I have subscribed this Extract and caused append my seal of office hereto. Given at Edinburgh the fifteenth day of July and of the Reign of our sovereign Lord King William the ninth year of 1697. ALEX R. ARESKINE, LYON."

Originally, the motto, as seen on an old seal, was

I FORCE NAE FREEN

I FEAR NAE FOE

It was translated into Latin by one of Captain Farquharson's ancestors, and henceforth appeared on the coat of arms as "Fide et Fortitudine". Surely the family insignia is the part of the regalia which has the deepest meaning and contains within itself the history of the clan.

History cries out too in the collection of warlike accoutrements, each lovingly handled by Captain Farquharson as he passed them to me. There was a powder horn made from a cow's horn of Invercauld. The filling end is fashioned in silver and set with an oblong cairngorm, while the other end is set with a thistle-shaped amethyst with a silver pin for priming the pistol. Then the pistols themselves, a pair of duelling pistols both customarily worn on the left side of the belt and made by the gunsmith G. Pratt about 1750. The barrels are finely chased with priming rods running along the barrel. At a later date a thistle cairngorm was added as an ornament. A wide leather cross-belt, which goes over the shoulder rather like the modern army's Sam Browne, holds at the left side a broadsword of burnished steel. On the right side goes the dirk. Its handle is of carved wood in a rope design and lies in a leather scabbard. The dirk is the early fighting knife. Its smaller knife and fork are a refinement of later days. The skeandhu, the black knife, is also a dagger and always worn in the stocking top of the right leg. The Farquharson skeandhu has a deer-horn handle and the family crest carved in silver on a black leather scabbard.

Then we talked about Highland dress. The Laird told me that most of his kilts are old, inherited from his grandfather, faded and differing in quality. A plaid goes with each kilt, all hand-fringed.

The sett of the clan tartan has deep blue background with a wide overcheck in green and two narrow overchecks in yellow and red. The dress tartan has a white sett. Captain Farquharson then showed me an exquisite plaid brooch which he wears on the left shoulder when in full Highland dress at a grand ball. It dates from the beginning of last century and consists of one large central cairngorm with six smaller cairngorms surrounding it in a delicate setting. The stones are intricately cut and give off lights like diamonds. His evening sporran is about 18 inches long, made from silvery-white goat hair and does not look its 150 years. It carried six long tassels of the same goat hair and the top mounting is of silver bearing the crest. The ordinary daytime sporran is made of short baby sealskin, has only three tassels and is engraved with the lion holding the dagger in the right paw. "If I wear a doublet and a lace fall I wear the old sporran, or a lawn fall with belt and short sporran."

As we passed up the great staircase to the upper hall lined with portraits of ancestors I stopped at one oil-painting. James Ross Farquharson, 12th Laird of Invercauld and great, great grandfather of my present host, looked down. Over his shoulder was a wide leather cross-belt, a sword at the left side. A waist belt held at one side a dirk, at the other a pair of pistols and a horn on which an oblong cairngorm was mounted. His sporran of goat hair had six silver-topped tassels, the silver mount bearing the Farquharson crest. He was in fact wearing the self-same objects I had been admiring in the library. But they were no longer show pieces to be turned over in the hand. They emerged from a living past and seemed to bring alive in the portrait the identity of the man who wore them.

James Ross Farquharson was the son of Captain James Ross R.N. who married Catherine Farquharson of Invercauld. She had succeeded to the estates and chiefship in 1806, and, on marrying her, Captain Ross took the name of Farquharson. In this portrait of the 12th Laird, painted by his brother-in-law Sir Francis Grant, his plaid is the Ross tartan which is red and green with an overcheck in deep blue.

At the top of the stairs the hall is like a friendly lived-in museum abounding in historic relics. The heavy beamed ceiling is off-set by the stained-glass windows which bear the coat of arms. At one side of the mediaeval fireplace hangs a black and white print, taken from an oil painting, of Lady Mackintosh, one of the daughters of

John Farquharson, 9th Laird of Invercauld. Captain Farquharson related to me the following story about Lady Mackintosh. She had married the Mackintosh of Mackintosh of Clan Chattan and was greatly attached to the cause of Bonnie Prince Charlie. She levied a regiment of fighting men, and wearing a man's bonnet on her head, a tartan jacket richly laced and pistols at her waist, saved the Prince from being taken prisoner at Moy Hall in 1745. To mark his gratitude Prince Charles gave to her a piece of his plaid and the ribbon from the Order of the Garter, and these mementoes are at Invercauld still. When she and her husband met after her raising of the Clan for the Prince it is said that the following laconic colloquy took place.

Lady Mackintosh: Your servant, Captain.

Her husband: Your servant, Colonel.

After which salutation she was generally known as "Colonel Anne".

Captain Farquharson recalled another story about the spirited lady. At a ball she was asked by a Royalist "Will you do me the honour of the first dance?" She agreed, providing "You will return the favour later on." When the time came for the return dance she instructed the band to play a famous Jacobite tune, "The Auld Stuart's Back Again" and her partner couldn't get out of it. The original oil painting hangs at Moy Hall. He added, "When the picture was cleaned recently a miniature of Prince Charles Edward was revealed in the bosom of her dress."

Many portraits adorn the walls — Francis Farquharson of Monaltrie (known as Baron Ban) who was taken prisoner at Culloden and did not return to Scotland until twenty years later when he spent his time making roads and building bridges; under his portrait is the sword he used in battle. Lady Amelia Sinclair who married James Farquharson of Invercauld in 1753 did much to promote the welfare of her tenants by introducing the little spinning wheel to Deeside for the preparation of linen yarn, and gave great impetus to cattle rearing. Her armchair, beautifully restored, stands near her portrait. Most poignant is the carefully preserved Order of General Wade instructing the Farquharsons to hand over in two weeks all weapons — poignards, dirks, pistols and guns. He gave them from 22nd September 1725 to 8th October, "to avoid pains and penalties".

In the elegant drawing-room small cabinets stand in the rounded windows hung with century old cretonnes. Here is a collection of strangely assorted souvenirs, miniatures of the Farquharsons of Monaltrie, a snuff-mull, a Masonic Order, a large square brooch of rose diamonds said to have belonged to the Countess of Moray, wife of the Bonnie Earl of Moray, a medal struck to celebrate Prince Charles' landing in Scotland. A strand of fair hair confirms that the Prince was indeed blonde and the gold locket which holds it reads, "This locket contains the hair of James Son, James 9th his consort and their sons Charles Edward and Henry 1745".

The Farquharsons rallying point of the supporters of the 1745 Rebellion is not far from Invercauld. You go down the valley to Inver Inn and the new bridge just beyond. Between the river and the hill is a clump of pine and larch trees and a pile of stones. Here the orders for battle were given. Each clansman contributed a stone in order to form a cairn. After the battle the survivors returned and each took away one stone from the cairn. What was left spelt the number of those who had fallen. It is called The Cairn of Remembrance. The slogan or rallying call of the Clan is the Gaelic for Cairn of Remembrance — CARN NA CUIMHNE.

Before I left the House of Invercauld I turned up Captain Farquharson's photograph in the Book of the Braemar Gathering of 1956 and asked him to describe exactly what he was wearing in this picture. Not strictly "regalia" perhaps but each item significant in its way. He wears a sprig of Scots fir in his bonnet. Each clan emblem should basically be a plant which is indigenous to the countryside of the clan. His doublet is dark sea-green tweed with deer-horn buttons, and his waistcoat yellow. Over the blue, red and green of the Farquharson kilt is the sporran made from wild cat fur, the paws forming the tassels. Silver kilt-pin and silver mounting for a plain skeandhu worn in the light coloured stocking top. His Cromach is of mountain ash with sheep's horn forming the crook on which is carved the likeness of the wild cat of the Farquharson country.

Chapter 5

The Black Sheep of Dinnet

MRS Frances Farquharson, wife of the 16th Laird of Invercauld, whose unforgettable family regalia I have described, has established the Invercauld Galleries at Braemar in a building which was once a Masonic Lodge. Built about 1870 it is situated where the road forks on its way south to the Devil's Elbow. Immediately opposite is the delightful granite cottage where Robert Louis Stevenson is said (according to the plaque affixed to the wall) to have spent the summer of 1881 and to have written his first great work *Treasure Island*.

During the last war, Mrs Farquharson, before her marriage, edited *Harper's Bazaar* and was Fashion Editor for *Vogue* magazine and she carries her feeling for colours and design into her ventures. She is vital, charming, indefatigable. She designed the décor for the nearby Braemar Castle, recently refurbished; she organises a Health and Beauty Shop and a Speciality Shop in Braemar; she founded in 1953 a theatre in the disused "Auld Kirk" facing the Invercauld Arms Hotel in Braemar where in summer are enacted plays, film shows, musical evenings and fashion shows. She searches up and down the country for people who excel at all kinds of Scottish art and craft and exhibits and sells their handiwork in this gracious gallery with its tall arched windows and lofty rooms. There I met Mrs Farquharson, dressed in the clan tartan, who enthusiastically showed me a 200 year old patchwork quilt and a quilted octagonal patch bedspread of today made by a lady in Ballater, wine glasses hand-engraved with grouse and pheasant, tartans of silk or of mohair, game record books bound in deerskin, leaded stained glass butterflies and flowers, cromachs with crooks of ram's horn, hand knitted pullovers with thick stockings to match, cowhide belts with Celtic symbols, tweeds dyed from heather flowers by an old lady who lives in Dunkeld.

"This silver platter" she explained "is engraved with the

Farquharson Lion from the Invercauld Coat of Arms".

An ancient loom stands in one corner of the showroom down-stairs, large and cumbersome but still usable, while a small staff of local weavers make tweeds on the smaller looms under the scrutiny of visitors. The tweeds are of beautiful and unusual combinations — pink and orange or green and blue and turquoise — and of course the more sober lovats and moorits, greys and browns. "This is my favourite", Mrs Farquharson confided to me, "this herring-bone tweed woven from the wool of the Black Welsh Mountain Sheep — Do you know the story? Lady Muriel Barclay-Harvey of Dinnet bought three or four of these black sheep many years ago from a friend in Hampshire. From this nucleus she bred at the Home Farm of Dinnet one of the largest flocks in Britain. Many of the materials woven on the premises here are of the black wool culled from this flock."

"Do you send your goods abroad?"

"I had a wonderful order for this same herring-bone tweed from a firm in New York. They wanted 500 yards and gave me a delivery deadline! I found girls in the North and in the Western Isles prepared to do the carding and spinning of the wool by hand and two weavers devoted two months at the looms in order to get the bales of cloth to the airport on time. Even so we only managed 480 yards! But it was accepted."

"What was the tweed to be used for?"

"Mostly for men's sports jackets — black mixed with a little white Cheviot".

I had heard that Lady Muriel's show rams had won the Supreme Hill Breed Wool Championship at the Royal Show at Kenilworth. These were the sheep!

So fascinating was her tale that I determined to investigate further the presence of the Black Welsh Mountain Sheep on Deeside and to fill in the gap between black lamb and black tweed!

I set out on a day in late spring when our interminable winter seemed at last to be securely behind us. First I called at St. James's Deeside Gallery at Dinnet where the enthusiastic owner, John Harrower, in addition to his collection of fine Scottish paintings of moors and pheasants, stags and rivers, offered for sale many beautiful objects hand-made in the north-east. St. James's, which is also his home, stands well back from the road and, hedged by the fragrant Rosa Rugosa, is surrounded by magnificent old trees like the Noble Fir and the abundantly flowering wild gean. From him I purchased a black and white checked blanket, soft and sweet smelling, woven from a mixture of Black Welsh Mountain wool and of white Cheviot — obtained he said from Lady Muriel Barclay-Harvey.

The North Deeside Road westwards from Dinnet village is bordered on either side by a woodland of thick straight firs giving way to lush green pastures at the approach to the farm with the black doors — The Home Farm of Dinnet — The freshly-leaved seedlings of silver birch lit up the panorama of the bare purple-brown hills behind. Through the branches of the pine trees slipped the first glimpse of the blue watered Loch Kinord on which the sun always seems to shine. Over its groups of prehistoric man-made crannogs the black-headed gulls glided silently. The banks of the loch were white starred with wood anemones under the bristling yellow gorse, junipers and snowy hawthorn. In the field in the foreground between loch and road a flock of pure black sheep grazed — ewes with their gawky lambs. Even at that distance the lustre of the dense black wool seemed to ripple in the sunlight. The young lambs leapt in the air with the joy of living. A prettier sight you couldn't imagine.

What to do next? Of course — call on Lady Muriel. There were notices along the private drive to Dinnet House which warned "Beware of Sheep", so I was not surprised to see a party of these elegant little creatures feeding on the grass fronting the imposing late 19th century mansion when she welcomed me into her home. She said her flock now consisted of about 375 ewes, 410 labmbs and 15 rams.

"I attribute the success of the black sheep here to the similarity of the Scottish countryside and the mountains of their native Wales. They are beautiful and not prone to disease in the same way as white sheep when we keep them in these natural wild conditions."

"I suppose they can fend for themselves?"

"One of the chief assets of the breed is that it fattens well on poor land without extra food to bring it through the winter."

"How often do the ewes lamb?"

"I breed from last year's lamb, known as a hogget when it has one offspring. In the second year it will have twins."

"How long before the ewes become mutton?"

"Four years at most. Four years is an old woman."

"Only at lambing time do the sheep see grass?"

"Yes, they stay at the lochside until they are clipped. Then they go up to the hill heather of Morven for eleven months of the year."

Lady Muriel suggested I should talk to Jack Crawford, farm manager at the Home Farm where the sheep-shearing was in progress. A group of the handsome horned rams were penned ready for the removal of their thick woollen winter coats. The grieve already had one ram tucked between his knees and was expertly removing the fleece with electric shears. I asked Jack Crawford if there was a precise moment for the clipping.

"You must wait for the new wool to grow, then run the shears in between the new and the old wool. It's important that the sheep are not on the hill at this time for the heather would catch and pull out the wool."

The grieve led out a four year old ram from the pen into the courtyard to pose for his photograph with Morven Hill in the background. The majestic creature had all the good points stipulated in the Flock Book of Black Welsh Mountain Sheep — a masculine wedge-shaped head, broad muzzle and forehead, prominent bright eyes, well curved horns and of course the black, short, thick wool containing no coarse rough hairs.

Mr Crawford confirmed that, because the sheep were more widely spread on the hillside, living on fresh air and heather, virus infection was unknown. He added, "If you start molly-coddling, they get diseases, like humans."

The attraction of this wool is that the colour never fades. The products — tweeds and blankets — are the natural undyed shades of deep brown and black and are superior to other cloths where warmth and wear are concerned.

I had yet to see the cloth being made. My next port of call was the 300 year old Knockando Wool Mill a few miles from Craigellachie in Morayshire. The Mill lies in a miniature green valley in the distillery country and the Knockando Burn ripples past the Mill where many years ago the water-wheel supplied the power. A twisting road lined with sycamores and red-berried rowan led to the Mill and the notice — A. Smith and Son, Manufacturers. Brown hens pecked by the burnside and oyster-catchers whistled overhead. When I entered the building I thought I was in a museum — a Victorian spinning wheel, a carding machine dated 1919 and a Dobcross Loom almost 100 years old, but no one in sight. I called out "Hello" and an answering voice came from inside the loom. Duncan Stewart, barely visible, was sitting on a cross-bar of the loom "tying on a new web". Almost 80 years old, and nephew of the previous owners, he disentangled himself and confirmed what I had already guessed. The woollen weft threads on the old loom were Black Welsh Mountain which had come, via the Wool Marketing Board, from Lady Muriel's flock at Dinnet.

The checked blanket took shape before my eyes. Eight pounds of wool are needed for one blanket. The wool after being washed to remove the natural grease is teased, carded, spun and finally woven.

"If nothing goes wrong, the weaving takes no more than three quarters of an hour. We wash the blankets and hang them out to dry."

Out on the green beyond the Mill the newly washed blankets had been stretched on wooden frames called tenters. These tenters have rows of hooks along both top and bottom battens to grip and hold the cloth. "That's the origin," said Mr Stewart, "of the expression — 'to be on tenterhooks'. Now you see these teasels. They're grown and harvested in Suffolk. The dried seed-cases — burrs we call them — are covered with sharp hooked husks like kittens' tiny claws, and we fit rows of these burrs into the raiser machine. As the blanket or tweed revolves the teasels brush and tease and raise the nap."

"That's the finishing touch?"

"Aye."

Knockando is the oldest wool mill working in this country today. A few years after my visit Duncan Stewart decided that after a life spent at the looms it was time to retire. It looked as if the Mill, active since the early 1700s, would have to close. But the situation was saved by two energetic young Londoners Hugh Jones and Robert Coffey who came to Scotland to learn the weaving trade. They offered to take over the Mill and with the guidance of the original craftsman are now carding, spinning, weaving on the same Victorian machinery.

The story of the Black Sheep of Dinnet is not quite complete. A member of a party visiting Dinnet House for the shooting was an American, Thomas G. Wyman of Maryland. He was so enchanted with the appearance of the sturdy gambolling little sheep feeding by the lochside that he asked Lady Muriel what chance there might be of exporting some to his farm in Maryland. Lady Muriel was agreeable and entrusted Jack Crawford to make the arrangements. The export of sheep direct from this country to America is

not permitted, but it may be done by transport initially to Eire —
in this instance 22 ewe hoggets and 2 rams from Dinnet to a farm in
the lovely Lusmagh countryside along the Shannon River. After a
period of quarantine, licences were granted and the progeny of
this consignment crossed the Atlantic.

Not long afterwards Lady Muriel returned to her English home
— Uffington House in Lincolnshire (where later she died in
September 1980). The affairs of the estate were looked after by the
Trustees and gradually the flock at Dinnet were dispersed among
farmers in other parts of Scotland. The ewes were crossed with
Dorset Horn rams and although the resultant lambs were fatter
and larger they were not so pretty! As an economic hill breed,
living on fresh air and heather, they have vanished from this area.

Jack Crawford is now working on his account as a Farming
Management Consultant near Monymusk. I went to see him at his
newly restored 5-acre croft by the roadside, recognisable at once
by the massed floribunda roses on either side of the entrance. He
has a great love for horses, and he and his wife are directors of the
Hayfield Driving School. He trains and breaks young horses for
riding, and "rests" old ones which are past their working life. In
the pasture I was introduced to "Austin Maxi", a beautiful
yearling Hafflinger stallion with chestnut coat and flaxen mane
and a retired mare of 33 years who keeps him company.

Has Jack Crawford lost interest in black sheep? Far from it. He
has just returned from a visit to Maryland at the invitation of Mr
Wyman. "Come and tell me if I'm doing anything wrong".

Speeding along the free-ways south from New York, past miles
and miles of wooden shacks and billboards and hot-dog stalls, you
come to the 4-mile long Bay Bridge, built they say so that oil
magnates could have country houses in Maryland. Here the scene
rapidly changes. Beyond the bridge along the shores of Chesapeake Bay are the fertile farming plantations on tiny peninsulas
stretching out into the sea, visited by colonies of thousands of
Canada geese. Mr Wyman's 600 acre plantation is on such a
peninsula, in March green with lush grass and magnificent old
trees. His home is a Colonial-style porticoed building with wide
windows looking across the sea and the fields where his flock of
Black Welsh Mountain sheep graze.

This breed is indeed hardy and healthy. At lambing time in
February they face daytime temperatures of 90° in the shade,

falling to 8° below zero at night. They're pure bred, not another sheep on the place.

"You're doing nothing wrong," said Jack Crawford, "but you're just a wee bit generous with your artificial feed. And now let's look at the rams and I'll tell you which are the best to breed from".

It's nice to think that when the President is tired of political affairs at Washington's White House he can sail the presidential yacht down Chesapeake Bay and see on his left hand side the Black Sheep of Dinnet.

How satisfying if things came full circle and descendants of the original flock came back to Deeside!

Chapter 6

James McGivern Humphrey, MC

ABOYNE has lost a warm and generous figure of military bearing in the passing of Colonel James McGivern Humphrey.

Born in 1892 in Saint John, New Brunswick, Canada he could trace his forebears back to the year 1655 when three brothers Humphrey took formal possession of extensive properties in the county of Fermanagh in Ireland. Towards the end of the 18th century his great-grandfather emigrated from there to Canada where the family settled. His father William — one of a family of four sons and three daughters — and his mother Elizabeth provided a happy quiet home life holidaying with the children every summer in a cottage on the shore of Saint John River. The young Jim Humphrey grew up in a Christian and church-going atmosphere, loving the country pursuits of walking, trout-fishing, picnicking, gardening and appreciating the growth of plants and trees.

When war with Germany was declared by Britain on 4th August 1914 Canada was automatically brought in. James Humphrey enlisted and attended an officers' training course, to be accepted as a lieutenant in the 87th Battalion of the Canadian Grenadier Guards.

After trench warfare instruction at Aldershot and Bramshott in Surrey his battalion reached the Ypres Salient where he was severely wounded. In 1918 during operations at Marchipont on the Belgian border he displayed conspicuous gallantry and resource for which he was awarded the Military Cross.

Many visits to England and to Scotland included Dinnet House on Deeside, the home of his old friend Sir Malcolm Barclay-Harvey, his wife Joan and daughter Violet. In June 1937 Jim Humphrey and Violet were married at St. Mark's Church in

Mayfair. A year later their son and heir Marcus was born.

On the outbreak of World War II in 1939 he was appointed Overseas Director of Auxiliary Services in London, being promoted to the rank of Colonel in 1945.

In the summer of 1947, he went to Scotland with his wife and son and spent a holiday at Dinnet House with Violet's father and her step-mother Lady Muriel Barclay-Harvey. Lady Muriel was responsible for the breeding of the Black Sheep of Dinnet described in my previous chapter. He was so impressed with Deeside, its beautiful trees and rich vegetation that two years later he closed his business affairs in Montreal, sold his house and set sail for Aberdeenshire.

He and Violet made straight for Deeside — Marcus by this time having gone to a Prep School near Oxford — and they were lucky to lease a furnished house, an old converted inn overlooking the River Dee. This was Norton House in Kincardine O'Neil belonging to Mrs Ursula Vaughan-Lee. There they lived for five years and entered whole heartedly into the activities of the district. The Colonel became Chairman of the Local Branch of the British Legion and of the Unionist and Conservative Association. Because of his military background he was appointed company commander of the local Home Guard.

As the house was near the river this meant salmon fishing from February to October. There was grouse, pheasant and partridge shooting and all the new-to-him countryside to be explored. But the great joy was the garden. At Norton he could develop his interest in all types of gardening — flowers and fruit and flowering shrubs. He was delighted with the long season of growth in the North East of Scotland and found the Deeside soil, unlike the lime soil of Eastern Canada, ideal for raspberries and strawberries, azaleas and rhododendrons, herbaceous borders ten feet tall, and the January flowering snowdrops which are followed so closely by the early crocuses. This however was someone else's garden and perhaps he wasn't sorry when Mrs Vaughan-Lee indicated early in 1956 that she required the house for her own use.

Where to go? Although Violet, until their son was born, was heiress to the house and estate of Dinnet there was no dower house on the property. By a happy chance there came on the market in the winter of that year the small estate of Rhu-na-Haven near Aboyne. This is a beautiful granite mansion house standing in a clearing of stately beech trees, the lawns running down to the waters of the Dee. Designed in 1907 by the distinguished Scottish architect Sir Robert Lorimer who is celebrated for his design of the National War Memorial in Edinburgh, it is superbly built of pinkish rough hewn granite, displaying many of the charming characteristics of Lorimer's art — the semi-dormer windows with pretty gable-heads, hipped roof, covered loggia and grassed terraces. The name Rhu-na-Haven means "bend of the river". Colonel and Mrs Humphrey paid their first visit when the frost was sparkling on the silver birches and the deep snow was untrodden around the house. They looked over the winding river to the trees of the Forest of Glen Tanar and to the fishing pool where the river is joined by the Tanar Burn. They glimpsed the walled garden and its greenhouses. They wandered through the oak-panelled rooms and the french-windowed dining-room with its elegant stucco decoration and its corniced ceiling. They admired the carved wooden ceilings and the ornamental fireplaces. It's no wonder they lost their hearts to it. Their offer to purchase was accepted and in April 1956 Rhu-na-Haven became their home.

It was through his garden at Rhu-na-Haven that in 1974 I first met the Colonel, then in his early '80s. I had been asked to write an article about the garden for the Aberdeen magazine *Leopard*. In about twenty years he had wrought great changes and improvements and showed me around with pride and satisfaction.

The crazy-paving terrace outside the dining-room led to the rose-garden in the centre of which was a statue of Pan playing on his flute. The roses had to be protected by wire-netting against the ravages of the hungry roe deer (like the Queen Mother's at Birkhall). There was the deep salmon rose "Elizabeth of Glamis", "Alamein" the colour of the poppies of Flanders fields and the old Damask Rose 'York and Lancaster'. "Do you know the origin of this candy-striped red and white rose the 'York and Lancaster Rose'? Legend says it signifies the union in the 15th century of the devices of the two Royal Houses — the Lancastrians and the Yorkists, the Red Rose and the White Rose. The shrub was given to me by a Deeside rose enthusiast.

"This has been the great flowering year," he declared as we walked along the lily-bed planted against a back-cloth of blue delphiniums in front of a high wall to the east and adjoining the house. "One of my greatest joys in the garden is my collection of lilies. They come from all parts of Asia. The best-known perhaps

is this white Madonna or Annunciation Lily." The tall stems each
carried several heads of satiny chalice-shaped flowers, their scent
permeating the whole border. "Once upon a time its bulbs had a
reputation for healing wounds and internal disorders!"

"Where does this white and pink trumpet-shaped lily come
from?"

"The Regal Lily? From Western China. Introduced to this
country at the beginning of the century. They can still be found
growing wild in their thousands in the Min River Valley".

Further along the lily border was a group of aristocratic lilies
which came from another Far East country, Japan. I recognised
the Lilium auratum, the Golden-rayed lily, with the broad yellow
bands down the centre of each ivory petal and the purple blotches
on the inner surface. "That variety was first shown in Britain at a
London Flower Show in 1862. Its neighbour also comes from
Japan, the pure white Easter Lily. Sometimes it has as many as
twelve flowers on the one stalk. Excellent for anyone starting a
collection as it's so hardy".

Scattered throughout the border were clusters of the delicate
rose pink lily Alstroemeria also called the Herb lily. "That's the
most gorgeous thing in the garden. There's nothing to compete
with it."

Against the south-facing wall of the house just beyond the
dining-room bay window grew a magnolia tree, the variety
Soulangeana which is unusual in the frosty climate of the North
East. The flowers — white with a touch of lavender. The Colonel
said, "I give it special care! A French viscount advised me to
mulch the roots with moist tea-leaves — then I'd have a prize-
winner! So I just empty the tea-pot over the soil and I have two
whole weeks' fragrant flowering."

As we passed the Japanese Umbrella Cherry Tree which in
spring is like a lacy parasole, a shower of fragile pale pink blossom,
I was halted by the melodious ringing of a bell. "That's the
Tibetan Temple Bell. On our world tour in 1968 we visited friends
in Katmandu in the Himalayan Kingdom of Nepal. I brought the
bell back with me".

"What's it for now?"

"It's a summons to the garden-boy to come in for his 11 o'clock
'fly-cup'."

Two delicate leaden figures guarded the shallow flight of stone
steps past the spreading rose-purple weigela to the "grassy gar-

den". One is Spring, a butterfly on her arm. The other is Summer, a garland of flowers in a halo over her head. We crossed the grass to the walled garden entered by a wrought iron gate, clematis montana rubens climbing up the stone gate-posts. "This was my own design," explained the Colonel, "I chose three emblems of Canada — the Beavers, Maple leaves and arrows. I gave my sketches to a German blacksmith at Dyce who fashioned the gate in his smithy." I was to learn more about the artistic side of my host's character later on.

Apart from the central path lined with hybrid tea-roses, violets, peonies and gladioli the walled garden was devoted to fruit and vegetables. Rhu-na-Haven was, and is, self-sufficient, and is renowned for its cordon-trained fruit trees — apples, pears, quince, plums and greengages — and of course raspberries, strawberries, red, white and black currants. "I keep, you see them there sheltered behind this hedge, the hives of bees essential to pollinate the fruits. But for jam-making I have a very special plum tree called Mirabelle, its fruits no larger than a sweet cherry."

"You don't find the Mirabelle often in this part of the country?"

"No, it comes from the Ardennes in the North East of France. Two specimens were shipped to me here by way of Leith and arrived safely wrapped in masses of straw.

Come and see my two favourites. First the Peach House. No artificial heat here, just nature's sun-rays through the glass to ripen the crop. It's the Peregrine peach tree. Plentiful. Perfumed. Comes from strong stock which is half the battle. The only protection in winter is a coverlet of straw over the roots."

Then we walked through the rows of peas and parsnips, Brussels sprouts, globe artichokes, parsley and spinach to the Geranium House. Ascending a wall trellis were bright pink and mauve geraniums and in front a pot-plant of oddly shaped and highly coloured blooms. "This is my great triumph" the Colonel said, "The Bird of Paradise Lily. The flowers look like the bird taking flight over the swamps of its native Cape of Good Hope. In South Africa pollinated by sun-birds.

It's five years old. Bloomed the first season and then not again until this year — the great flowering year."

His love of the garden equalled his love of the church. Every Sunday morning he attended with his wife sitting in the front pew in one of the loveliest little churches in Scotland — the silvery granite Scottish Episcopal Church of Saint Thomas in Aboyne. He

sat below the plaque erected in loving memory of Baroness Glen
Tanar, esteemed wife of the founder of the church. The Colonel
greatly helped the church through his generosity and felt strongly
in favour of the union of churches of different denominations. It's
not surprising therefore that he combined love of garden and love
of church in one grand Garden Fete.

In the spring of 1977 he drew up plans for the opening of the
Garden on 7th May at Rhu-na-Haven when by mutual agreement
the congregations of two churches — St. Machar's Presbyterian
Church and St. Thomas' Episcopal Church, both of Aboyne,
promised to participate. We were all roped in. Meetings were held
in his library for the allocation of jobs — designing the posters,
printing the tickets, collecting flowers, baking cakes. Tea to be
provided in the Badminton Hall to the east of the house. Volun-
teers to pick daffodils and narcissi growing so abundantly under
the trees throughout the grounds. Little girls in party frocks to sell
made-up posies of polyanthus and forget-me-not. Bookstalls,
pot-plants, barbecues, pony-rides for the children, fly-casting
competitions on the river. An insurance to be taken out in case of
rain. And the great and novel attraction — the Royal Marines
Brass Band from London.

We prayed for the sun. It rained. It descended in a deluge, but
no one's spirit was dampened. We hung tarpaulins over the stalls.
The Royal Marines fled to the stables where they set up their
music again. And over it all the kindly presence of the Colonel in
tweed ulster and tweed cap. We made £1,000 divided equally
between the funds of the two churches.

In his autobiography *The Golden Bridge of Memoirs* published in
Canada a year before he died he mentions casually, "Some years
ago my wife and I took up painting in oils with modest success".
Around the walls of the library are examples of his work — scenes
on Deeside, Loch Kinord, his own garden, views of Nepal. He
took with him his paints and canvasses whenever he went on
holiday.

Ian Strachan, art teacher at Aboyne Academy, inaugurated a
series of evening classes in 1962. He said, "We had a painting class
of twelve in the former A.R.P. hut, where the gas-masks used to
be distributed during the last war, opposite the little cemetery on
the approach road to Aboyne Castle. It's a substantial building
with a shingle roof kept cosy by an ancient coke stove. Colonel and
Mrs Humphrey were among the members — mostly ladies from

Aboyne and roundabout. The happiest crew I had anything to do with. Wonderful atmosphere."

In autumn and winter they sat at their easels in the hut. In spring and summer they went on painting excursions to the Moor of Dinnet, the Queen's Loch, the Fungle braving the hordes of biting midges. They sketched too with charcoal and pastel and produced work of a very high standard. How did the Colonel show up as an artist?

"He exhibited a joy and enthusiasm which you might expect in a younger person. He had a meticulous and painstaking approach to painting. He would carry in his head an idea of some thing he'd seen — the sun setting over Morven Hill perhaps — and, better than words, he'd translate into pigment whenever he got home. Landscapes were always his choice — tree plantations, mountains, rivers, fields, peaceful scenes but painted with zest and strong yellows, red and vivid greens."

"The interpretation of his subjects was always factual?"

"When I suggested to him an abstract form of painting he just laughed so kindly — 'No thank you very much'.

Every year we held an exhibition of the season's paintings in the hut, open to the friends of members of the class — tea and sausage rolls and the best silver. We'd great fun!"

I returned to Rhu-na-Haven last September and Violet Humphrey walked with me round the garden. Little was changed. The Cox's Orange Pippins were ripening, the sweet peas were eight feet high, clumps of autumn crocus lit up the borders, the black "parson" rabbit had set up his home deep in a grassy bank. And in the hot house the Bird of Paradise lily now flowers every year.

Over the fireplace in the Colonel's drawing-room hangs another example of his appreciation of art — the magnificent painting by John Spurling of the famous tea-clipper *Thermopylae* with in the background her keen rival *Cutty Sark*. Whole forests of timber, fir and oak, were floated down the River Dee last century to Aberdeen ship-builders from Glen Tanar, from the very forests that can be seen from Rhu-na-Haven garden. *Thermopylae*, launched in 1868, was a fine example of the craftsmanship of the ship-builder Walter Hood of Aberdeen. The painting of this beautiful ship the Colonel had espied during the last war in a shop in London. The following day the shop was bombed and one of the few things still intact was *Thermopylae*. Feeling it was destined for him he bought it for £20!

Although the Colonel had been a soldier serving his country with honour throughout two world wars, he was at heart a man of peace. He had no belief in the so-called glamour of war, seeing only its futility.

Before he died in 1979 at the age of 87 he wrote these words as a preface to his book, quoted here as an epilogue.

> A Man's life is a composite of all that he has done, all that he has dreamed and has made come true, and of those things which he can pass on to those who come after him. According to this definition, I have had a good life, a life I can recall in all its various aspects with satisfaction. And now, in its eventide, I can look back and reflect that I have done my small part in trying to shape what will be a better world, not only for future generations of Humphreys, but for all mankind.

Chapter 7

James Craig, Blacksmith

BEAUTIFUL wrought iron work is to be found all over the
North East — the garden gate at Rhu-na-Haven, the gates at
Birkhall and Balmoral, Dunecht House entrance railings, ploughs
and harrows, inn-signs, hanging swees — all made at a time when
blacksmiths combined the shoeing of farm horses with decorative
iron work.

I thought I would pay a visit to James Craig whose smiddy on
the North Deeside Road at Drumoak ten miles west of Aberdeen is
well-known to every passing commuter hurrying home to supper.
It's a lovely little hamlet. First I passed a group of modern County
Council houses on my right set back from an apron of newly mown
grass immense beech trees lining the road. Almost opposite were
the iron gates of the east entrance to the stately neo-classic mansion
Park House designed by Aberdeen architect Archibald Simpson
in the early 19th century. Further west old dormer-windowed
cottages, embroidered with lupins and snow-in-summer, looked
out upon a stretch of sycamore and oak and beech. And then Park
Smithy, over a hundred years old, a long low granite building and
above the doorway the brilliantly coloured Royal Coat of Arms, by
appointment to Her Majesty the Queen in recognition of his work
carried out at Balmoral.

In the courtyard in front stood a magnificent 12-ton canopied
steam-roller, painted glossy red and black and yellow, and standing back admiringly, a polishing cloth in his hand, was James
Craig. Approaching seventy, a mighty man, every inch a blacksmith, with great strong arms and humorous face he had been at
Drumoak since 1947. The steam-roller? "I bocht her fae a scrap-
yard in Peterhead thirteen years ago for £140 and reconditioned
and repainted her."

"What's it worth today?"

"Maybe £10,000. At one time you could buy an aul' steam
engine for £25 that could fetch £12,000 at auction noo. From scrap
to gold as you might say."

The brass decoration certainly gleamed like gold and the name-
plate bore the name *Eileen.*

"Why Eileen?"

"I named her after my dochter."

On the forks over the front roller were two most elegant paraffin
lamps. Mr Craig bought them "a' black an' greasy" from an
antique shop in Banchory for £4 apiece. Impatient to see what they
were, he stopped on the way home and "gave them a scrapie".
Brass!

That same evening he took sandpaper to the lamps till they
glowed like fire. "I couldn't sleep a' night for brass dust up my
nose," and he added proudly "you should see her when she's fully
dressed, with her lamps on!"

Now in as perfect working order as when she was made in 1926
by John Fowler of Leeds, *Eileen* has passed the Boiler Inspector's
test. Three rallies he has driven her to in 1980 — at Hazlehead,
New Byth and Maryculter, the Gala for B.P. at Dyce and the
Alford Cavalcade. At Alford she won the Shield for the Best Steam
Engine of the year.

In the background was a Scammell Highwayman Tractor, a big
monster built in 1953 — "This is what takes *Eileen* about loaded
on a long trailer — down to Stirling for a gala." Following in his
father's footsteps, James Craig's son did up the tractor and painted
with lots of coats of red paint with hand-drawn gold lines. "When
she's a' bonny cleaned up she's lovely!"

"Are these heavy steam rollers still made today?" "Na," he
replied with scorn, "it's a' they light weight yellow diesel engines
now to roll the tarmacadam. The front wheel's got to be filled with
water as ballast. No fire to light, no steam to raise. Jist press a
button and away ye are to work. It used to be a pretty rough job
steering and watching the water gauge on the boiler but it was
quiet to drive and we used coal, coke or wood — anything that
would burn."

There aren't many smiddies in full production nowadays.
They've become no more than curiosities to interest the summer
visitor. Mr Craig used to make estate gates, fire-baskets, wrought
iron hinges, rod springs and, of course, he shod the horses that
farmers brought in to him. But now the tractor's taken over from
the horse though there is a revival in horse-riding.

"Thirty years ago I kept two to five men. Their wages were 3/6
an hour. Today a farrier can earn at least £2 an hour. Bit a' my men

have gone to the oil-rigs to find the "black gold". So I'm on my own."

The inside of the forge was lit by the smouldering glow of the furnace or "smithy hearth" as it is called. Around were all the tools of his trade. The old anvil, 276lbs in weight, was made in 1926 and would have cost a £5 note. It was set up on a blackened log with, as he struck it, "a rare ring on it". There was the power hammer for sharpening picks, the turning lathe, welders, power saws. He was working on "an aul' fashioned set o' fire dogs" for one of the big Deeside houses, the sparks showering off the anvil at every blow of the hammer. "How long will it take you to make?" "One long day, aboot ten hours." It was already taking shape, the beautiful turned scrolls curving downwards to form splayed feet embossed with arrow heads.

Although the roof of the smithy was fairly low, I saw in the dimness at the far end what looked like a little room tucked high up under the ceiling. "Aye, that's the wee bedroom where the farriers used to sleep. The bed was along the gable wall. Ye see the wee shelf fixed to the wall? That's where the alarm clock stood within reach o' the sleeper's hand."

"How did they get up there?"

"By a stairway they hauled up by a pulley."

Long ago part of the smithy was a byre — usually for two cows and a calf, and there was a communicating door to the cottage.

Mr Craig showed me another interesting feature — the door facing the road. Built like a stable door in two halves it still carried the original hinge-bands, bolts and ancient lock with heavy key. "They were all hand-made by the blacksmith here afore me. Though the wood's beginning to rot and splinter I canna bear to replace it."

He led me outside to see some of the other things he loved, his collection of old agricultural implements.

A mowing-machine, dating back to 1918, with a three foot cut, stood in the field. It had two seats at different heights, one for the man driving the horses, the other for the man tilting the grain on to the blades. Next to the mower lay a hand-plough, called a "man and wife". The man held it, the wife pulled!

Among his oldest treasures is a one-horse gear and threshing mill. The horse, by walking in a circle, drove the belt connected to the machinery of the mill. Built in 1876, the mill is a rare piece with hand-made wooden roller and spokes for threshing the corn.

If the horse wasn't available the threshing could be done by hand, working a handle at either side of the mill. In the old days, Mr Craig added, "They aye threshed on a Sunday".

Still in the field I almost tripped over a smiler rake. I asked "Why smiler?"

"If ye did a day o' that ye couldna' smile!"

Safely under lock and key, a Lucas's "King of the Road Lamp" maybe off a steam-waggon at the turn of the century: a paraffin flare lamp which was used to light the stalls on market days at the Castlegate in Aberdeen; a blacksmith's bellows. My favourite was the governess cart, in service during the 1st World War, but now needing "redding-up". The two big wheels, 4½ feet in diameter to make it "easy pulled", were rusty and worn. The face-to-face seats at the sides had lost their fine upholstery, and the basket-work seat-backs were torn and faded, but soon no doubt to be brought back to its pristine freshness.

Above his desk in his tiny office hangs a testimonial.

> ASSOCIATED BLACKSMITHS' SOCIETY
> This is to certify that James W. Craig was admitted a Member of the Above Society in 1933.

Around the text are pictured all the different aspects of the blacksmith's trade, which he has followed for almost half a century. James Craig is one of the old school, a craftsman, a race that is fast disappearing, with his love for the traditional way of life and its romantic keepsakes.

"And when, or if, you retire?"

"Weel I could retire bit I'll aye keep my hand in."

I'd already seen the ornamental flower stand he had made for the West Church of Banchory gifted this year in memory of a parishioner's parents. "A lot of scroll work on it," he went on. "A bonny thing, a strong made thing. Retire? Ach ye're better to work. Fit wid I dae jist walking aboot the streets o' Bunkry?"

Chapter 8

Lavinia Smiley of Castle Fraser

AT about the same time that the blacksmith's treasures of
transport were bowling along the country roads — the steam
rollers and governess carts — there could be seen proceeding in
stately fashion from Dunecht to Aberdeen the yellow Rolls Royce
limousines of the 1st Viscount Cowdray. I remember well seeing
the Rolls driven down Albyn Place by a liveried chauffeur with
Viscountess Cowdray sitting erect in the back seat in Queen Mary
style toque and cape.

Lord Cowdray of Dunecht and of Cowdray Park in Sussex
acquired the 2,000 acre estate of Castle Fraser at Sauchen near
Kemnay in 1921. He later made over the estate to his son the Hon.
Clive Pearson who in turn passed it on in 1946 to his daughter
Lavinia and her husband Major Michael Smiley.

Castle Fraser, one of the castles of the Earldom of Mar, is a
superb example of the fifty or so Z-plan castles built in Scotland
towards the end of the 16th and the beginning of the 17th
centuries. It was designed and constructed by Andrew Lord
Fraser and his master mason I. Bell, one of a family of masons
responsible for many north east castles in the Scottish castellated
tradition. The Frasers, after whom the castle was named, were of
French origin, the name Fraser deriving from "fraises" meaning
strawberry. The 5-petalled flowers of this fruit may indeed be seen
chiselled in stone in the coat-of-arms over the castle door. The
interior has been beautifully preserved and restored for the
Smileys by the Hon. Clive Pearson and the late Dr Kelly of
Aberdeen.

Major Michael Smiley, a serious and successful farmer, grows
mainly barley crops for the distilleries for malting of a high
standard which is sold in bulk to Grampian Grain Ltd. in Aberdeen and also abroad. As for cattle he specialises in the pure bred
French Charolais and has one of the largest herds in Scotland. One
of Her Majesty the Queen's trustees for the Balmoral Estate, he

was recently awarded the CVO in recognition of his services.

I motored there last winter when thick snow was on the ground, twenty miles north east cross country from Aboyne. I chose the longest entrance drive where the drifts were deepest and my little yellow "Beetle" skimmed lightly over the frozen surface. And suddenly my first view of the pinnacled fairy-tale castle arising out of the snows — a fantasy of embattled parapets, two-storey corner turrets, steep crow-stepped roofs, dormer windows with carved stone gablets, and entrance archway flanked by two little gate houses all set in a sparkling silent parkland of massive ancient oak trees.

But it wasn't the castle I had come to see but the stables! Built to the west of the castle on the rising ground beyond the Ducat Park the stable court was the creation in the late 18th century of the then laird Miss Elyza Fraser. It was designed in the form of a hexagon with a conical tower at each corner around a paved courtyard. The impression is that of an old French farmhouse in the Loire. I entered through an arch where the carriages used to pass after setting down the owners at the castle doorway. There I was met by Lavinia Smiley of many talents — author, artist and prime mover in the conversion of the stable buildings into the most delightful residence for her own and her family's use.

What were once the coach-house and harness room have become the entrance hall. Where the stalls for the horses once stood is an elegant dining-room. The hay-loft above has been transformed into the drawing-room, now home of Louis XV furniture and 18th century paintings, and the lumber room and granary have blossomed into pretty four-poster bedrooms.

This fascinatingly shaped house is only one room wide, the upper floor being reached by spiral staircases within the corner towers. The stairs are now fitted with soft red carpet and the narrow gunloop windows in the depth of the tower walls are double-glazed, the walls so thick there is space to stand a piece of porcelain between the two panes of glass.

Mrs Smiley took me first to see the dining-room where the carriage horses once lived and ate and slept. The only horse now seen there is the model in silver of the race horse "Cottager" on the handsome Hepplewhite sideboard. Rich green hessian covers the walls. Doors, ceiling and cornice are pure white, the cornice having the egg and dart motif representing life and death. At the windows hang floor-length curtains of white cotton satin, edged with white braid, lined with primrose yellow and, most practical point, interlined with old blankets. The circular table is covered with a yellow linen cloth which has a bowl of white Christmas roses and silver partridges in the centre. Individual strip lights illuminate the pictures. Outstanding is the magnificent Italian oil-painting of a country scene with a shepherd boy and girl in the foreground, river, ruined temple and mountain in the background. It was painted by Locatelli in the late 17th century.

The bedrooms are small but highly individual. The "David Garrick" room looks as if it had stepped straight out of the 18th century. The suite of furniture comprises a four-poster bed with slender reeded posts and a canopy of finely scalloped wood and valance of green satin. Dressing-table, bergère chair and small commode are painted with stylised scenic designs. A very old patchwork quilt lies over the bed. The suite, given to Mrs Smiley by her great aunt Mrs Gertrude Kinnell, is in fact a modern copy of furniture made especially for David Garrick the actor. The originals may be seen in the Victoria and Albert Museum.

Next to the nursery. My hostess grew up in the 1920's with her two sisters Veronica and Dione in an atmosphere of nannies, governesses and nursery teas at Parham in Sussex, Grosvenor Square and Dunecht House in Aberdeenshire so it follows that in the stables conversion one room was put aside as a nursery for succeeding generations of children and grandchildren. The table was already laid with animal iced biscuits and fruit cake in one of the prettiest rooms in the house with white walls, red Turkey carpet, rocking chairs, children's furniture, flowered chintz curtains and cupboards still overbrimming with toys. Mrs Smiley collects 18th century needlework pictures and early Victorian colour prints which adorn the walls. She is herself expert at making montages and over the fireplace is an example of her work, a Victorian group whose flouncy dresses are made of real brocade, the curtains of damask and the tiny pictures within the picture are real paintings.

When a visitor enters the nursery she shuts the door, not realising there are five doors in the same wall and all different colours. On making an exit the bewildered visitor tries every door in turn to the delight of any children who happen to be present. I suffered the same fate!

Finally to the drawing-room, the erstwhile hay-loft, which has a simple cottage fireplace painted white in keeping with the rough-cast plaster walls. Heavy yellow silk curtains under richly pleated swags frame the windows. Most unusual is the Sheraton mahogany oval library table. Each drawer is marked with "alphabet labels" or groups of letters of a filing system — ABC, DEF and so on. This is sometimes called a Rent Collector's Table.

The whole of the conversion reflects the personality of the owner — her taste for what is beautiful and her choice of gentle happy sunshine colours.

Seated on a deep sofa upholstered in yellow damask in front of a roaring log fire, large vodka and tomato juice in hand, I heard about Lavinia Smiley's plans for her new book entitled *A Nice Clean Plate*, a light hearted account of her childhood during the years between 1919 and 1931 with her young sisters.

Why does the book have that title?

As children, the author admitted they had "Everything that Money Can Buy". She said simply, "My grandfather had made a large fortune." They lived in a big corner house looking out onto Grosvenor Square in the West End of London, and had what she called a "tremendously privileged and sheltered life". One of the disadvantages perhaps was that they were expected to eat a great deal, more than they wanted — lots of porridge, bread and butter, hot buttered toast, rice pudding, ground rice, sago, tapioca (frogs' eyes), macaroni and golden syrup, 'spotted dog', treacle tart rounded off with regular doses of Cod Liver Oil and Malt! Nannies knew in those days that the more you could persuade a child to eat the stronger it would grow. So the constant encouragement was to, "Make a Nice Clean Plate". The result, alas, was that they grew rather fat.

Summer holidays were often spent at Dunecht. By train from Kings Cross Station to Aberdeen where Rolls-Royce taxis waited to drive the party to Dunecht. She remembered that first breakfast on their arrival — eggs and bacon and sausages, and herrings fried in oatmeal and heather honey spread on baps. It was breakfast to the strains of the bagpipes drifting in at the windows, the piper walking slowly between the herbaceous borders in the garden. While staying there they found great pleasure in wearing the green and black Dunecht Tweed, the same as all the retainers — keepers, ghillies, gardeners and the groom who looked after the two Shetland ponies Spick and Span who drew the little open carriage.

In spite of the wealth of the family the three Pearson girls were taught to be thrifty in their financial dealings. Their pocket money for years was 5/- a month and they were taken by their Nanny to Williams Deacon's Bank in Pall Mall to collect it. A serious man in a black coat would ask them in turn how they would like their money. It took them ages to make up their minds. Dione, the youngest, often chose hers in pennies or halfpennies, while Veronica and Lavinia preferred the more sophisticated coinage of sixpences or silver threepenny bits. The serious cashier never allowed a flicker of a smile to cross his face during these transactions.

The children had to account for every penny spent, each in a thin red marbled cash book. Their father would sit at the nursery table with them, going over the entries such as "Pencil Sharpener", "Put in box, for Waifs and Strays" or "Present for Nanny". It was a very good training which no doubt stood them in good stead in later life.

This is one of the most charming books I have read.

In 1978 the National Trust for Scotland published her book *Life at Castle Fraser 150 years ago* compiled from documents in the Charter Room at the Castle. As in *A Nice Clean Plate*, it is written with her characteristic liveliness, compassion and humour, recounting the joys and achievements and tragedies of that family. On the front cover is a reproduction of a pencil drawing of Castle Fraser made in 1829 by the Aberdeen painter James Giles, a great friend of the Fraser family and frequent visitor to the Castle. The last Fraser laird was Theodora, widow of Colonel Frederick Mackenzie Fraser. Of her Mrs Smiley comments in the closing sentence of her book, "She sold the Castle with many of its contents, to my grandfather in 1921 and went to live in England in a warmer climate."

In lighter vein is her production of a series of seven attractive little books written and illustrated by her for the five year olds. An accomplished artist, she says that her hobby is drawing and painting people's houses in water-colours and then having the drawings reduced to postcard size, like her pen and ink sketch of the fairy tale Castle Fraser itself.

In 1976 a new chapter began in the history of Castle Fraser. Exactly 400 years after the Royal Arms were set up on the south wall of the Castle, which was at that time no more than a fortified tower, the property passed into the care of the National Trust for Scotland along with an endowment for its upkeep from Major and

Mrs Smiley. The year 1981 was the Golden Jubilee of the Trust and to celebrate the occasion the firm of James Cocker and Sons, Rose Specialists of Aberdeen, produced a new rich gold Hybrid Tea Rose called Golden Jubilee. A bed of these roses was ceremoniously planted on Sunday November 15 within the old 2½ acre garden at the Castle — the high warm red brick walled garden where Lavinia aged twelve used to play and pick the flowers. Dick Hillson, Assistant Director of the Grampian Region of the Trust, officiated in the presence of Aberdeen Lord Provost Alex Collie, the Smileys and Mrs Anne Cocker, managing partner of the firm.

An appropriate coincidence. The creator of the Golden Jubilee Rose was Mrs Cocker's husband, the late Alex Cocker head of the firm of Rose Specialists. His great grandfather was James Cocker who in 1840 was head gardener — where? At Castle Fraser. His employer Colonel Charles Fraser, demanded that he worked on a Sunday gathering fruit in the walled garden but, as a keen observer of the Sabbath, this he refused to do. A quarrel was the result. James Cocker left the Castle and headed for Aberdeen where he founded the now famous firm of James Cocker and Sons.

As a by-product of her restorations at Castle Fraser Lavinia Smiley has brought things full circle with the re-introduction of the name of Cocker into the old world garden.

Chapter 9

Anne Cocker — Rose Specialist

JAMES Cocker, head gardener at Castle Fraser, quarrelled in 1840 with his employer about picking fruit on a Sunday. He said that he would gather the fruit on Saturday night, no matter how late, but not on a Sunday. The outcome was that James Cocker left Castle Fraser and started a nursery business at Sunnypark in Aberdeen (an area now built up with council houses), concentrating on the production of forest trees and herbaceous plants.

The firm has grown and expanded through almost a century and a half, each generation of Cockers taking charge in turn, specialising finally in the breeding of high quality roses. They opened further, but temporary, nurseries at Morningfield in King's Gate, Springhill and Muirfield in Langstracht on the western outskirts of the city. A permanent and perfect site for growing roses was finally acquired in 1959 at Whitemyres still further west on the Langstracht — a total of 138 acres.

The rose has been with us a long time.

The gossamer pink-white Damask Rose whose fossilised remains were discovered recently dates back to the living fragrant flower of three million years ago.

Shakespeare wrote about it. Redouté painted it. Poets have sung its praises. John Gerard eulogised it in his 'Herball'. The Chinese have grown roses for countless centuries. Dried bouquets of wild roses have been found in Egyptian tombs placed there as a last offering.

Yet, strangely, the art of rose cultivation from its wild ancestor is only two or three centuries old. Aberdeenshire has always excelled in the cultivator's art. Rose specialists and nurserymen and enthusiasts in their own back gardens take advantage of the fertility of the soil, the soft quality of the rain and the clear unpolluted atmosphere to increase the production of this magnificent flower a million-fold.

Whitemyres is ideally situated for this purpose lying on the border of the city's 'Green Belt' with the land sloping to the south. Whitemyres House, built about 1774 and immediately adjacent to the rose-nursery, was acquired in 1962 by the late Alec Cocker when it was still in a sad state of dereliction, having been left empty for about thirty years. During the long period of neglect the harling flaked from the outer walls, the slates slithered to the ground, woodworm took over in the woodwork and the steps of the staircase crumbled and fell apart. Mr Cocker restored and extended the house and Mrs Cocker was responsible for the planning of the décor throughout transforming it into a gracious and beautifully proportioned house now scheduled as a Georgian building of architectural interest.

When I visited Whitemyres a few months ago I was greeted initially by a family of tawny pea-hens strutting proudly up the beech bordered avenue calling to their lustrous peacock master and disappearing among the rhododendrons and desfontania. Mrs Cocker invited me into the sun-room, part of the new extension, a stylish conservatory housing an umbrella tree from Java, a Mexican breadfruit plant and an ivory pineapple from Brazil.

She was looking sunburnt, being newly returned from Israel after attending the 5th World Rose Convention organised by the Royal Horticultural Rose Society. I had not thought of Israel as a source of roses.

"They don't do terribly well in gardens because of the lack of water. But they're grown under glass commercially for the cut flower market and are supplied to the florists, social functions and even to Britain out of season. They're cultivated near the Sea of Galilee where there's very little rain and are watered by trickle irrigation to the rose beds before the sun gets up."

"Did you make a holiday out of your trip?"

"After the Convention we went south along the Valley of Jordan, verdant country producing melons, avocados, olives, all the citrus fruits. In November when we were there the sun shone all the time — warm, lovely evenings."

"Will you go back?"

"My ambition is to grow a new cut flower variety and sell it to Israel."

"As Managing Partner of the firm what does that entail?"

1. *Delgatie Castle as it would have looked at the time of the Crimean War.*

2. *Lillias Conn aged 18. Taken from a water colour by Mrs Rachel Grant Duff of Delgatie.*

Via Marsilles

Via Marsilles

(Y.)

Miss Lillias Conn

Delgaty Castle by Turriff

Aberdeenshire Scotland

3. and 4. *Envelope and letter addressed to Lillias Conn by her brother in 1855.*

3/2806 Heights before Sebastopol

4

July 31st 18

Dear Sister   I received your letter of
29th of June and I was glad to hear by it
you are all in good health as this few li
leaves me enjoying part of the same j
we are always under fire of the enemy
there is no hopes of being any o
way only we belive there is another a
Attack on the 21st of Agust and th
is four of the 79th 600 of the 42 and
of the 93rd all for the Storming party or
forlorn hope So I dont some of will ha
a bad chance of ever returning to
Scotland again I had a very narr
escape on the 14th at about eleven
they made a determined Sortie and
Regiment was lying in the advan
trench the night was very dark a

Bitter market there I bought a new
shirt 6/6 a dozen of shirt buttons for
2/- 2 nedles for 6d a hank of thread for
4d so you may guess how things sells
in this part of the world I wish you
to put your adress on your letters as
that is the way they would let you
know if I was hurt or Killed for our
lives is not insured here nor we dont
know the minute we may get the
head nocked off I shall add no
more at this time give my kind love
to aunt Betsey and all enquiring
freinds and I remain your and
affectionate Brother George Conn

3932 Pte George Conn
1st Company 79th Highld
British army in the
Crimea

Via Marsilles

5. *Birkhall — The Queen Mother's Scottish Residence.*

6. *The Border of pink Windsor phlox in front of Birkhall.*

7. *Jock and Mary Esson.*

8. *The Farmhouse at Wester Micras.*

9. *Jock Esson as a young man in the late 1920's when he was fee'd as a shepherd at Auchtavan.*

10. *Captain and Mrs Farquharson of Invercauld at Invercauld Castle.*

11. *The brilliant yellow saddle cloth, over 100 years old, hand embroidered with the coat-of-arms of the Farquharsons.*

12.	*The Herd of Black Welsh Mountain Sheep by Loch Kinord near Dinnet.*

13.	*The four year old Welsh Mountain ram.*

14. *Duncan Stewart (left) with Hugh Jones beside the old loom at Knockando Woollen Mill.*

15. *Rhu-na-Haven in springtime.*

16. *Colonel James M. Humphrey.*

17. *Exterior of the smiddy at Drumoak.*

18. *The magnificent steam-roller at Drumoak named 'Eileen'.*

19. *James Craig, blacksmith, at work.*
20. *A drawing of Castle Fraser by Lavinia Smiley.*

21. *The converted stables at Castle Fraser from the courtyard.*

22. *The dining-room at Castle Fraser stables which originally housed the horses.*

23. *Outside the drawing-room at Birkhall on the occasion of the handing over of the Crathes Castle Roses to the Queen Mother. Pictured with Her Majesty are Dick Hillson assistant director of the National Trust for Scotland (Grampian Region), Douglas McDonald head gardener at Crathes Castle, Anne Cocker, Anne Murray and Jenny Hillson.*

24. *The beautiful Silver Jubilee Rose.*

25. *The exterior of Cocky Hunter's Store in Castle Terrace in 1955.*

26. *Alex Hunter — Cocky Hunter the Second.*

27. *Bill Hunter and his wife cutting the cake at their Golden Wedding in 1978.*

28. *Balbithan House, Kintore.*

29. *The Garden at Balbithan.*

30. *Mary McMurtrie having tea in the garden.*

31. *Jessie Kesson (left) with the author at the BBC in 1950.*

32.   George Barron (right) with two other judges Tom Brayshaw and Mrs Helen Chalmers at the Britain in Bloom Competition looking at Bill Laing's garden in Campsie Place, Aberdeen.

33.   The 17th Century Great Garden of Pitmedden where George Barron was head gardener until 1978.

34. *James Hird in his Council House Garden at Summerhill.*

35. *A corner of James Hird's garden.*

36. *Peter Kaminskas, the gardener, at Bellenden, Milltimber.*

37. *Bessie Brown, sitting in her garden at Heatherdale Cottage near Banchory.*

38. *Walter Leiper, the lapidarist, at his grinding machine in Garlogie School.*

39. *The old school and school-house where Walter Leiper has his gem-stone cutting business.*

40. *Harold Esslemont photographing Alpine plants in the Swiss Mountains.*

41. *My father, H. Adair Nelson, in the garden at 65 Osborne Place in 1922 before setting out for the theatre in the evening.*

42. *Family group of the Adair Nelsons taken in 1921 — self, Peggy, Hal, my mother and Bill.*

43.   The interior of His Majesty's Theatre in 1957, the 'Watteau' curtain already replaced by the red velvet drapes.

44.   The exterior of His Majesty's Theatre, Aberdeen taken in 1906 the year the theatre opened. Schoolhill Railway Station and Black's Buildings on the right (since demolished).

45.   *Les Fêtes Venitiennes by Watteau on which was based the painting on the theatre curtain called The Minuet.*

"I look after the office work and the hybridising while my son Alexander, who has just celebrated his 21st birthday, is a partner organising the work in the fields. I have a staff of twenty, two double-span greenhouses and we recently put up a plastic tunnel."

"Tell me about the hybridising."

"First, I lay down the programme. We do the pollination in the greenhouse experimenting by crossing the pollen of the best and strongest flowers after studying their pedigrees. You never know what the result will be by this method of propagation. That's part of the fascination. Two reds wont necessarily produce another red — it could be pink, yellow or white. At the end of the year when the blooms have faded we gather and open up the ripened hips, take out the seeds and put them straight into a sand mixture. I keep them indoors, varying the temperature to break the dormancy. In fact I fool them into thinking it's time to wake up! In early spring a seed bed consisting of a compost of sand and vermiculite is prepared. I select the best seedlings — they have an incredibly quick growth in June and July. From those that look good we take the bud wood and graft it into the briar stock already growing in the field."

"Where do you get your briar?"

"From Holland. I tried English briar but I'm happier with Dutch. It's a wild briar called Rosa Laxa. I order 300,000 a year."

"And then?"

"A year afterwards — that is the following summer — I look at them in the field for disease resistance, health, brilliance of colour, formation of flower, habit of plant and foliage and lastly perfume."

"Can you breed perfume?"

"Oh no. Perfume comes along as a bonus."

"Then you build up your stock?"

"I keep increasing till I have enough to put out into the fields for sale and despatch perhaps as many as 10,000 roses of one variety."

"How long would it take — from seed to perfect flower?"

"About seven years."

Much of the enthusiasm in rose culture and hybridisation was inspired by Napoleon's Empress Josephine towards the end of the 18th century. At the Château of Malmaison in France Josephine assembled a unique collection of roses in her glorious garden — new varieties sent from countries abroad even from Egypt during Napoleon's campaign. There flourished the yellow Scotch rose, the thorny Cabbage rose of a hundred pink petals, the purple velvet Van-Eeden, the crimson Bengal rose, the brilliantly striped Bourbon roses, Rugosa red and white, the Crested Moss rose (known also as Châpeau de Napoleon), the fragrant Noisette of which there may be a hundred blooms successively in one season, white washed with pink, clustered at the ends of the down-covered stalks. Her roses were immortalised by the great flower painter of the age Pierre-Joseph Redouté, delicately and accurately recorded for coming generations of rose-lovers. There were two hundred and fifty varieties at Malmaison most of which are in our gardens and our breeders' glass houses today.

So it is with pleasure that we see in the Cocker brochure the names of the old Species roses, the Bourbons, the Rugosas, in addition to their latest award-winning creations. Illustrated in color on the front of their 1981-82 catalogue is one of the new roses called Crathes Castle, a pure pink silken floribunda in the foreground, behind — a glimpse of the world famous garden established by the late Sir James Burnett of Leys, and towering over all, the magnificent Jacobean Crathes Castle. In the top right hand corner of the picture is the Royal Coat of Arms — By Appointment to Her Majesty Queen Elizabeth II.

Cockers have supplied roses to the Royal Gardens for many years. To celebrate the 80th birthday of the Queen Mother in 1980 the National Trust for Scotland desired to present to her as Patron of the Trust twenty five Crathes Castle roses for the garden at her Deeside home of Birkhall.

Anne Cocker explained, "The Representatives of the Trust, Douglas McDonald, head gardener of Crathes and I were invited to Birkhall for the informal ceremony of handing over the gift. Her Majesty, after making a symbolic planting of one rose-tree, entertained us to tea in the drawing-room and Douglas Westland of Inverurie took a souvenir photograph of us all outside the french window."

Supreme of all the roses is the creation of Alec Cocker's — the hybrid tea Silver Jubilee. It has a pedigree that can be traced back 150 years. The description in the brochure reads:

> The established trees are seldom without flower and are beautifully clad in mid-green glossy foliage down to ground level. The colour is a confection of pink, apricot, peach and cream. Every bloom comes in perfect shape and form.

How does it attain these qualities?

Mrs Cocker explained, "My husband was responsible for breeding these qualities in the greenhouse seven years ago. The immediate parents of Silver Jubilee are the coral pink Mischief which contributed strength and the unusual pyramid shaped bloom, the red rambling rose Parkdirektor Riggers which brought the hardy disease-free genes of the Rosa Kordesii family, and Piccadilly whose perfect buds are bright scarlet on the inside and gold on the outside."

She showed me the "Family Tree", like that of a noble family, the famous antecedents each furnishing in turn unique characteristics — the ruffle edged cream and pink hybrid tea Peace, the wild magenta Rosa Rugosa, Noisette and Bourbon which derive from a Chinese strain, the fertile Karl Herbst, the vermilion Super Star, Gallica and Species roses — all these and many more have come together to make the aristocrat Silver Jubilee. Already it has won the International Trophy and Gold Medal for the best new rose of the Royal National Rose Society's Trials.

"My husband died just before his rose was launched and it was left to me to see it out into the world. Her Majesty Queen Elizabth graciously granted permission for us to use the name Silver Jubilee to commemorate in 1977 the twenty-five years of her reign. Among the first plantings were a bed of fifty of these roses in the Balmoral Castle gardens that year."

"Your husband would have been very happy with the success of his rose."

"Yes, we produced 125,000 bushes for the trade alone. His work has been made everlasting in another way. The makers of fine porcelain, Boehms of Malvern, have manufactured a group of Silver Jubilee roses, designed by Diane Lewis — in full bloom with pointed buds and deep green foliage."

She brought it for me to see and stood it on the table. Hand-painted, the petals were as delicate as the living flower.

"Only three hundred were made. I sent down to Malvern the real roses as models. Queen Elizabeth was presented with the first one. The second came to me. I shall buy a display cabinet specially for it.

And now I must prepare for the Chelsea Flower Show."

Chapter 10

Cocky Hunter

THE theme for this book is that of the personal endeavour of North East Folk past and present — of soldiers, farmers, gardeners, writers, rose-breeders. Now I turn to a story of a different sort, the dealer in second-hand furniture.

Among the many legendary landmarks which are so quickly being eroded in Aberdeen must surely be included the disappearance of that much loved furniture store known affectionately for generations as Cocky Hunter's.

The original "Cocky" (so named because of his smart dapper appearance in which he took great pride) was born Thomas Hunter in 1867 in Water Lane off Virginia Street, overlooking the harbour. Leaving school at the age of thirteen he took a job with a fish-dealer called Mary Fletcher and with the aid of a pony and two-wheeled cart used to stock up with speldings from the tiny fishing villages between Aberdeen and Collieston. Wages 1/6 (7½ new pence) a week! Later he went into a shipyard and became a boiler-maker, transferring to a similar job in West Hartlepool where he met the woman who became his wife.

Women were tough in those days. She bore him sixteen children, was 18 stone in weight, worked from 8 a.m. to 8 p.m. every day and lived to the age of eighty-six. On their return to Aberdeen Cocky opened his first second-hand furniture store in East North Street in 1903. Every market day they would load a hand-cart with goods at 4 a.m. to push to the market in the Castlegate, boasting that whatever the weather they never missed a market.

By 1908 the results of their hard work enabled them to open a further shop in Commerce Street where he remained until his death in 1925. Cocky, good-natured and kindly, was known as the man who bought and sold anything "from a needle to an anchor". These Bargain Stores offered furniture of all kinds and doors, windows, paint, grates, baths, cycles, radios — an endless variety. Aberdeen children used to chant

"If you want a knocker for yer door,
Or a hoose tae fit yer floor
Ging tae Cocky Hunter's Store
In Aiberdeen."

Customers used to bet one another that they could get the better of the old man and asked for the most ludicrous things. One local demanded half a loaf of bread. By a coincidence Cocky had brought in a half-loaf for his morning piece, so over the counter it was sold. Another time a pennyworth of the edible seaweed, dulse, was requested. As it happened that morning Old Betsy, the fisher-girl who walked the streets with a creel on her back selling buckies and tangles, had left at the store a "Pokie o' dulse" for the owner's supper. They never got the better of him!

Cocky had unusual pets who, when they weren't roaming free in the streets, were treated like members of the family. Buller the donkey, who supplemented his feed with snacks from the school kids and visits to Mitchell and Muill's the bakers, lived to an overfed eleven years. And Jacko the little brown monkey, stowaway on an Indian ship, caused fines to be imposed by the police for his mischievous tricks and thefts from the city shops.

Cocky the First died at the age of fifty-eight in 1925 and his popularity was reflected in the grandeur of his funeral. His coffin was carried by pall-bearers made up of boiler-makers along the streets densely crowded with mourners all the way from Commerce Street to Trinity Cemetery. The gates of the cemetery were kept open until dark so that his hundreds of friends, from civic dignitaries downwards, could file past the grave.

Soon most of his family had branched out on their own. Albert opened a furniture business in Gardener's Lane. Four daughters ran cycle, pram and other second hand goods depots in Castle Street, the Gallowgate, George Street and Queen Street. Cocky's youngest son Bill took over the premises at Commerce Street. His eldest son Alec, who inherited the title of Cocky, also branched out on his own, first as a cycle dealer in Exchequer Row and then as a furniture dealer in South Mount Street. In fact my first recollection of Cocky Hunter's dates back to the mid thirties when I was a member of Aberdeen Little Theatre Guild. This amateur repertory company presented a series of period and modern plays at His Majesty's Theatre and were produed by Moultrie Kelsall of broadcasting fame. I remember best *The Immortal Lady* by Clif-

ford Bax and J.M. Barrie's *What Every Woman Knows*. I not only
acted in these plays but also — as stage manager — was deputed to
choose antique furniture to dress the stage. And Cocky's in South
Mount Street was the place!

The building, 2½ acres in area, was, during the First World
War, occupied by Mortons, suppliers of tinned foods to the
Forces, and acquired by Alec Hunter in 1932. Because of the size
of the building, bounded on four sides by South Mount Street,
Leadside Road, Richmond Street and Kintore Place, everyone
scoffed at him, but the enterprise flourished and became the envy
of the second-hand trade throughout Scotland. To this old and
rambling structure Cocky brought treasures he discovered at
auctions, in private houses or sales of bankrupt stock and he filled
the 2½ acres, three floors of it, to bursting point. It was Aladdin's
cave. Ranged around the walls or piled high one on top of the other
with no space to pass between were brass bedsteads, cast-iron
grates, tripod walnut tables, Sheraton desks inlaid with sea-shells,
slender glass-fronted bookcases, rose-wood sewing tables with
ivory fittings and needlework bags, sets of decanters, settees with
dainty spindle backs, boxes of tools, bits of bicycles, cat's whisker
wirelesses, a room full of sewing-machines, reproductions — and
sometimes originals — of the Scottish landscape painter Joseph
Farquharson's snow and sheep scenes. Dangling from the ceilings
on hooks were Victorian nursing chairs, papier-mâché chairs
inlaid with mother-of-pearl, Regency chairs, Trafalgar chairs.
And the cost was next to nothing — £5 for a 19th century
Davenport, 3/- for the sewing-table, 10/- for a chair! But for the
Aberdeen Little Theatre Guild my choice of furniture was loaned
free of charge for which as a "thank you" we were glad to insert an
advertisement for Cocky's in the theatre programme.

For the young boy too it was Paradise. Able to wander about
unhindered he could find and purchase a clock that wanted its
hands, a motor for his Meccano or for only 2/6 an Edison
phonograph with the original black cylinder records — which
worked! The rickety wooden stair-cases, overflowing with pieces
of furniture, led to further floors each bending under the weight of
the "junk".

I used to think what a death-trap the building would be in a fire
— and a fire there was! In 1937 Cocky Hunter's was burnt down
and most of its contents destroyed. Alec and his family were living
at Nigg at the time in a house near Loch of Loirston and they were

called out in the early hours. As they drove in from the country they saw a great blaze in the sky like a sunset. The fire engines were there all day damping down the smouldering ruins while against the red glow were silhouetted figures of helpers carrying to safety tables, sofas and pictures down the outside stairway. But no-one was hurt.

On this site now stands the Rosemount Flats the first great block of municipal flats to be erected in the city, the curved exterior walls adorned with sculptures by T.B. Huxley-Jones.

What happened then? Cocky Hunter's didn't lie dormant for long. To explore the next chapter I was taken by my friend May Thomson who was for many years Assistant Librarian in the Reference Department at Aberdeen Public Library to meet Bill Hunter, brother of Alec, and his wife Jane at their fascinating house at No. 56 Castle Street. How often people pass this lovely row of granite houses, myself included, without a second glance. Although some of the buildings have certainly seen better days, each is individual in architecture, with beautifully proportioned windows, steep slated roofs, dormers and broad chimney stacks. No. 56 just west of the Bank of Scotland and immediately opposite the Town House, stands on the corner abutting the new Grandfare supermarket. Erected in 1763 it is one of the only two eighteenth century houses still in being in this the old market place of the city. It's a three storied ashlar building with attic and original and unusual bow dormers. To the east is the archway to Victoria Court pend. At one time this was the home of the Bursar of the University and was indeed called The Bursar's House. Today the ground floor is occupied by a public house named "The Welly Boot" an arched and fan-lit mahogany doorway leading upstairs to the Hunters' residence.

Bill and his pretty wife, now in their seventies, welcomed us into the comfortable kitchen/parlour of their house. They'd lived there for fifty years and incidentally had, last spring, celebrated their golden wedding with a fantastic party at the Carlton Rooms entertaining sixty-four guests to lunch.

May asked the questions and I wrote down the answers! In 1938, about a year after the disastrous fire Alec (Cocky the Second) acquired the huge building in Castle Terrace which had previously been the Sick Children's Hospital in Aberdeen. Originally a private house it was enlarged greatly when converted to a hospital. In spite of the addition of the corner balconies for the convalescent

children it must have been a depressing place for the young
invalids looking straight into the Castlehill Barracks.

A self taught expert on antique furniture, Persian rugs and
porcelain, Alec soon filled this shop too with treasures collected
from modest cottages, modern bungalows and country mansions.
In fact he filled the store literally to overflowing so that bicycles,
writing desks, tea-sets, wrought iron gates all spilled over onto the
balconies, pavements and granite setts of the roadway beyond —
to the consternation of the constabulary.

Among his customers he was proud to include the late Lady
Burnett of Leys who often commissioned him to buy antiques on
her behalf for Crathes Castle.

He had a special brand of humour. It amused him to place a
notice on a large coffin in the store which read, "Please do not lift
this lid". The customer invariably did so and screamed with
horror when a skeleton was revealed. "Another time" added Bill,
"my brother bought at an Old Meldrum roup a glass-sided hearse
and a grandfather clock. The natural place to put the clock was of
course lying flat inside the hearse. He drove carefully back to
Aberdeen. In those days traffic was controlled by policemen on
point duty, and when the cortège reached George Street, the
police, thinking it was a funeral, signalled a clear passage through
the traffic all the way to Castle Terrace, greatly to the delight of the
driver!"

In 1961, at the age of sixty-nine, Alec died having suffered from
ill-health for some years. But the legend lived on. His only scn
Tommy and several assistants carried on the business at Castle
Terrace, while Bill remained at Commerce Street.

Tommy now has a small second-hand furniture store in Spring
Garden. He too had a coffin story to relate. "After the war my
father bought thirty coffins from the A.R.P. and lined them up in
a row against the railings outside the store. A country joiner saw
them and bought the lot on condition that Cocky never divulged
what they were because he was going to make them into a bedroom
suite for his wife!"

However all good things it seems must bow to the winds of
change. A development firm, Avonside Properties Ltd., bought
Cocky Hunter's store at Castle Terrace and the disused Scandina-
vian Church behind intending to replace them with a 62,000 sq. ft.
office block. That was in 1972. Bill told me that during their last
days at Castle Terrace, rather than sell at a loss, they decided to

destroy their goods. "The stuff we broke! We took hammers to
break them up — wally dogs, tables, paraffin lamps, rocking
chairs. No one wanted old fashioned things like brass candlesticks
turning green. I got tuppence for them as scrap but only if I broke
out the interior metal. Otherwise I got only a penny." The
frustration was aggravated by the fact that still, although demoli-
tion had been carried out, the site stands empty, half hidden by
hoardings, office block not yet built.

A few years later another blow fell. The premises in Commerce
Street had to make way for that part of the new inner ring road
running from Virginia Street along Commerce Street to East
North Street. Bill's wife handed me the advertisement in the
Evening Express, May 23rd 1975.

> Cocky Hunters'
> Closing Down Sale
> Sat. First May 26
> Final Reductions.
> Mr and Mrs W. Hunter wish to take this opportunity to thank their
> many customers and friends, old and new, for their valued support
> during their years in business.
> Bargain Stores,
> Commerce Street.

After sixty-seven years!

Then the Hunters took May and myself next door into "The
Room". As in many Georgian houses the ceilings are lofty, the tall
narrow windows lighting up a beautiful drawing-room with pieces
of antique furniture no doubt selected from the Cocky Hunter's
stores — a walnut glass fronted bookcase which came from a big
house at Cults, solid brass flower-pot stands, a Rococo gold-
garlanded mirror and a pair of superb French porcelain painted
wall plaques which Bill assured me were 16th century.

But best of all, Bill said, in a showcase, beside the Crown Derby
and the Royal Doulton — a be-ribboned golden horseshoe from
their Golden Wedding Cake.

Postscript

In January 1981 Bill Hunter telephoned me to say he'd no
objection to my including in *North East Folk* this article on Cocky
Hunter previously published in Aberdeen Leopard. But did I
know that his wife Jane had just died?

Today January 8 1982 I learn that Bill died yesterday aged 75 —
"suddenly but very peacefully" — the service to be at his beautiful
home in 56 Castle Street, thereafter to Trinity Cemetery, resting
place of the original Cocky Hunter.

Chapter 11

Mrs Mary McMurtrie
of Balbithan

THE fact that I remember "Raggy Morrisons" and James
Mearns — one of the partners of Morrison's Economic Stores
of St. Nicholas Street, his counters laden with Indian silks, fine
nuns' veiling, Javanese cottons, shot taffetas, transparent voiles,
shimmering velvets, often bankrupt stock of high quality, the
prices seldom exceeding 1/11 per yard, the elderly but attentive
shop assistants dressed in black suits and white winged collars,
always polite to the jostling crowds seeking bargains — has really
nothing to do with my next subject.

Nothing whatever. Except that on the way to the House of
Balbithan near Kintore where lives Mrs Mary McMurtrie —
historian, artist, botanist, writer and gardener — at the side of the
small road coming down from the cross-roads are the ruined
foundations of a cottage and the remains of a little garden with
starry yellow Lesser Celandine in cushions around the tumbled
walls. The name of the cottage had been Croontree and it was there
that the legendary James Mearns (born in 1862) spent the early
part of his life with his parents. Of the same calibre and period as
Cocky Hunter, he must have made a fortune out of Raggy's for in
1922 he bought Aboyne Castle and Estate and became a County
Councillor for Aboyne and Birse. From cottage to castle! On his
death at the age of 81 in 1943 the castle reverted to the Marquess of
Huntly and the Economic Stores site along with the adjacent
Netherkirkgate and Flourmill Brae ultimately gave way to the
super store of Marks and Spencer.

Relics of past architecture are evident throughout our countryside — a cottage wall here, a mill-stone there, but nowhere so
much as in the castle or large house. Many mansions in the North
East dating back to the 16th and 17th centuries have been re-built,
windows blocked in, ceilings lowered, roofs heightened, great

fire-places re-discovered, halls divided into smaller rooms. So it is with Balbithan, barely six miles north east from Castle Fraser as the wild geese fly.

The forsaken cottage behind me, the descent to Balbithan took me past the Home Farm and into a sheltered little valley lined with flowering white gean trees and golden broom, opening into the avenue towards the lovely turretted house harled in creamy white. In the foreground spreading chestnuts and beech and a smooth wide lawn and clusters of snowy narcissi and forsythia. As I approached, the owner Mary McMurtrie emerged from the shrubbery, secateurs in hand. Pleased I think to have a respite from pruning and weeding she took me first to the herb garden protected from the breeze by a small yew hedge. There we sat and chatted among the pungent smelling cat-mint and feverfew and tansy. There were, too, beds of balm and apple mint and ginger mint and eau-de-Cologne mint — lovely names. "When I do cook I use some of them." There was the dainty pale pink soapwort too. "In the old days a lather was made from the roots and leaves for washing fine embroideries and laces." Her eyes twinkled — "Not the way I do my laundry!"

"How do you come to live at Balbithan?"

"Well, in 1960 I was just looking for a house in the country. I answered advertisements and saw lots of different houses but this seemed to be handed to me."

"What does the name Balbithan mean?"

"It has two translations — Town, or Place, of Birches and Beside the Boggy Stream and they're both accurate. I'll show you later."

Balbithan started life in 1560, no more than a stark tower house, standing alone amid what was then only bleak peat moss. It was built by the Chalmers family. They held the estate until the end of the 17th century and it has passed through many hands since then.

"And of course many alterations and extensions to the building?"

"Yes as you see Balbithan is now a large L-shaped house with a rectangular stair tower in the re-entrant. After 1630 it had become The New Place of Balbithan."

"What condition was it in when you bought it?"

"Oh not very good. There was dry-rot in several places. People thought I was mad, quite mad. Perhaps I was. I certainly didn't realise what I'd taken on."

"Did you receive any grants to help you?"

"The Historic Buildings Council made several grants to cover the eradication of the dry-rot and re-roofing. Also the walls were stripped and the stone work pointed and one staircase replaced. Under the Council's conditions the house is open to visitors by appointment.

I loved to watch the local craftsmen at work, as skilful I'm sure as the builders of old. I had massive oak doors made and the heavy iron hinges, the snecks and nails were all hand-made by the blacksmith of Kintore, Mr Strachan."

"Who was your architect?"

"The late A.G.R. MacKenzie, a near neighbour at Bourtie House, was responsible for the beginnning of the restoration. After his death Mr Mennie the Inverurie architect helped me. During the restoration several garderobes were found and re-opened.

Do you like bats? You see that cone-shaped roof on the turret? There are many little bats at the top of the spiral staircase inside."

"Would you call Balbithan a happy place?"

"Yes it has a happy atmosphere and I think you could say that history has passed lightly over Balbithan. Once during the Covenanting troubles it was plundered by Covenanting forces and Montrose is said to have made it a rendezvous where he met with his leaders. Later it was a refuge for Prince Charles's followers after Culloden."

"And Bonnie Prince Charlie himself?"

"It is a nice tradition and of course we would like to think he took shelter here, perhaps occupying a small room looking onto the garden but I am afraid he was never in this part of the country!"

"Shall we go round the garden now?"

"I've tried to re-create it as I think it may have been although no records of the original lay-out of the garden exist. I've stocked it with roses and herbs of the 18th and 19th centuries. The only definable remnants of the old garden were some straight paths like the one we're on now, a small orchard of apple and damson trees, an old oak and some ancient Irish yews."

"Where is the Great Beech of Balbithan mentioned in the Statistical Account?"

"Oh it was cut down many years ago but it was quite near the house. It must have been marvellous — a straight trunk twelve feet in circumference, branchless up to twenty-four feet, then seven boughs stretching up to fifty feet. But there is a fine old copper beech here now."

We walked down the garden path hedged to one side by Rosa Mundi, the striped rose which sometimes reverts to the magenta rose and beyond was a long raised bed of mixed Alpines. There was the anemone blanda — "it seeds itself, so many colours. In its native Turkey it grows among rocks and in woodland." Beside the anemone grew the tiny yellow saxifrage and the Alpine phloxes, the coarser lungwort purple and red, miniature daffodils, the little hoop-petticoat narcissus and dog-tooth violets. "I'm hoping to grow sweet scented violets. This is one of my favourites — Mountain Avens. It has a little oak leaf and white 8-petalled flowers, like clematis with its fluffy seeds. I'm sorry it's not in flower yet. The yew hedge at the end of the walk — I cut it myself, a great effort. It looks lovely later in the year, the red vine Tropaeolum twining up the deep green."

On the soil lay a small fork and a box half filled with weeds. "I've been struggling with weeds. It's hopeless.

This place had gone back when I came but there was an old herbaceous border and lots of currants and gooseberry bushes and the old rhododendrons. I kept some of the old Ponticum which had contorted stems and interesting shapes."

There now stretched a broad lawn with a pavement of flagstones in the centre around an old millstone supporting a brass sundial. The granite pillar of the sundial was once the working part of a grass-roller. Around the flagstones was a circle of the crimson-purple 'old velvet rose' or Tuscany.

"I wanted the garden to be full of surprises so I've divided it up into many little gardens by planting hedges of yew and of the old Scotch roses Spinosissima pink, white and yellow." The first surprise was a bed devoted to irises of every colour shown against a background of dark conifers. There were lilac streaked with yellow, inky blue spotted and striped, purest white, coppery orange. Dividing the bed was a series of stepping-stones. "I collected and laid them myself. I have to hunt for flat stones. This is boulder country so whenever I see a good flat stone I stop and pick it up."

Beyond the lawn were ornamental cherries, one especially fine, the Tibetan Prunus Serrula with trunk of gleaming copper. It was grown from an aerial graft taken from the magnificent specimen at Crathes Castle.

"These rhododendrons were raised from seed from the Royal Botanic Garden in Edinburgh over thirty years ago. Some haven't flowered yet. I'm eighty now. I'll never see the blossom. This is a frost hollow. Some plants hate the early morning sun — they just shrivel up and die."

Just around the corner was another surprise garden, a little pond prettily shaded by golden cypress and willow. Marsh marigolds clustered over the flat stones bordering the pond, some butter yellow, some white with yellow centres. "I must get the pond running again." We peered into the water, full of frogspawn. "The water's gravity fed down a pipe. When it's flowing it's lovely. I can just hear the trickle. The pipe is hidden in the ferns.

Before we go into the house come round and see the red trillium, it's in flower. It's a woodland plant, grows best in the semi-shade." The group of lily-like flowers had 3-petalled blooms of dark burning red. "See how the sun shines through the petals." Another little box of weeds and a trowel.

The grassy walk leading back to the house was lined with old gnarled apple trees. "They don't fruit nowadays but they look well with the white scented Seagull rose growing up them." We passed the Nursery where she propagates the herbs, laced and cottage pinks, Alpines of all kinds which are for sale to help meet the constantly increasing costs of maintenance.

"Over the wall it's a field of gold" and full of enthusiasm she took me round the side of the house and the old cheese press with the white Jacobite Rose growing beside it to her Golden field — a field of Lesser Celandine of brilliant star-shaped glossy petals lighting up the sombre shade under the silver birches. Meandering through the woodland a little stream under a narrow bridge, its sloping banks densely carpeted with the golden stars. "You see — this is the realisation of the name Balbithan — Town of Birches and Beside the Boggy Stream. This is one of my favourite spots. The Celandine is a wild flower not a weed. The word celandine comes from the Greek meaning a swallow. There's a legend that the flower was supposed to appear on the arrival of the swallows and to die at their departure." At the entrance to the celandine field before the little bridge grew a 40 feet high Balsam Poplar, the sticky coating of its buds sending a fragrance over all.

We went into the house by the Garden Room which had originally been a servants' hall, the low ceiling spanned by a heavy adzed beam. Then we mounted a narrow service stair curving up within the thickness of the wall to reach the Great Hall which is now used by Mrs McMurtrie as her library and her studio for painting. Spread over the octagonal table were some of her paintings, sketches, books of reference, manuscripts, jars of flowers, all the requisites for the work she is engaged upon. Her book is called *The Wild Flowers of Scotland*. Marc Ellington of Heritage Press at Towie Barclay Castle is the publisher. In addition to the text it will contain 17 colour plates of the delicate and detailed water-colours of the flowers she grows, or finds, and loves. Printed on special paper and hand-bound in leather, each volume will be signed by Mary McMurtrie, the publisher, papermaker, printer and binder.

At the window stood her easel, paint brushes and little wild flowers in bowls some from the Burn o'Vat on the Moor of Dinnet. "This is always where I do my painting because the window faces north west. Have you ever seen a reducing glass?" She carefully unwrapped from a silken handkerchief a glass not unlike a magnifier. "This shows me how my pictures will look when reduced in a book. It really is a treasure."

"Did you attend Art School?"

"Yes, I went to Gray's School of Art in Aberdeen. You were talking about Raggy Morrison. We, as students at Grays, used to buy bits of canvas at Raggy's for painting. The janitor made our stretchers and mounted the canvas and we sized them ourselves, a smelly pot of size heating on our cloakroom fire after classes were over. Raggy's was a marvellous shop for everything. You see those two Persian rugs? They came from Raggy's!"

Mrs McMurtrie led me to the long gallery on the floor above where are hung on the white walls paintings by two of her three daughters — Bettice Tessier, who lives in France, and Elspeth Haston. They specialise in landscapes. Visitors who come to see the house and garden have also the opportunity of admiring their work.

"How about tea and rock cakes?"

We went down to the paved patio where stone troughs were filled with alpines and miniature conifers and the roses climbing the wall near the oak front door and central turret were just coming into bud, the palest pink New Dawn and Madame Alfred Carrière, white with a faint blush. We sat, in the sunshine, tea-cups on a little Jacobean table. I asked her where she lived before coming to this wonderful place.

"For ten years in Aberdeen, before that at the Manse of Skene. My late husband was Minister there, our parish church at Skene was one of the 'small livings'. At that time Jessie Kesson, author of books and radio plays, was a young girl at the Skene Orphanage and she used to come to the Manse sometimes and show us the poems she'd written. She said she liked to listen to my husband talking and reading her poetry because he'd a beautiful voice."

"Did you know the dominie at the school?"

"Donald Murray? Oh yes, Jessie dedicated to him her now famous book *The White Bird Passes*."

We stayed chatting until the celandines under the balsam tree were closing their golden petals. When I got up to go she said, "I have enjoyed our afternoon. Now what shall I do after you've gone? I suppose I ought to do some house-work but it's such a bore isn't it! Write letters, painting, gardening?

Gardening I think."

Chapter 12

Jessie Kesson, Author

ALTHOUGH Mary McMurtie knew Jessie Kesson as a girl living at the Skene Orphanage and visiting the Manse for tea and 'poetry readings', I didn't meet her until her mid-twenties.

Jessie Kesson didn't need "discovering" but I did introduce her to B.B.C. Radio.

I had invited her to attend drama auditions at the Aberdeen Beechgrove Studios. She very nearly didn't come at all! With her husband Johnnie and two young children, Avril and Kenneth, she was living and working on a croft at Linksfield near Elgin in Morayshire when the typewritten invitation arrived. She tells me now that the envelope was opened with trepidation because typing meant officialdom! Most unwilling to spend the bus-fare from Elgin to Aberdeen on what might come to nothing, she was persuaded by Johnnie — for once throwing caution to the winds — who said "you just never know".

So she set off on foot along the railway line that ran past the cottage towards the station, pondering whether to spend the money on the bus-far or her cigarettes for the next day or two. The cigarettes won. She retraced her steps homeward along the railway track to confront a disappointed husband. "There's still time," he urged, "The auditions go on all day. Catch the next bus. You just never know".

At the studios, Moultrie Kelsall, as Senior Producer, was conducting the auditions. Jessie sat nervously awaiting her turn. Her description of him "The handsome Moultrie was of a species I had never encountered before. The end of a hard and maybe fruitless day glittered wearily in his eyes. His dark hair high and afloat, himself trying to bring it down with sharp staccato hands". Each script he offered her to read she handed back to him. No, she couldn't play the part of a grandmother or an old tipsy wifie. "What can you do then?" he barked. So she read Violet Jacob's poem *Tam in the Kirk* one of her favourites. He thanked her and walked her to the front door. When she got home she told an expectant Johnnie, "A waste of time. A waste of money. The Mannie just said 'thank you'".

But, out of that first encounter with Moultrie Kelsall arose a lasting friendship and respect for each other's talents.

Within a week she received a telegram from us asking her to write and read a poem in my radio production of Vincent Park's *Town and Gown.* She wrote a lovely poem *A Scarlet Gown* and that spelt the beginning of a long collaboration — she writing, I producing at least thirty features and plays on the Scottish Home Service.

I was asked recently how did I recognise at once the quality of Jessie Kesson and I answered that it was the beautiful phrases that came tumbling from her tongue and pen. Words like

> Knitting endless pink bed-stockings,
> His swash-ling panache, (Moultrie)
> What's going on behind your strange still face?
> The man who casts the invisible dice.

Phrases that conjure up whole situations, their colour and their setting, in a few words. But mostly it is her authenticity, her earthy humour, her honesty, her extraordinary memory and her deep deep feelings for her childhood, its hurts and its healing, that make this author outstanding.

From a presentation of love poems and songs in 1947 called "Till a' the Seas Gang Dry" in which Kenneth McKellar made, I believe, his first professional radio appearance singing "Oh my luve's like a red, red rose", she wrote many scripts portraying facets of her early life of poverty spent in the wynds and alleys of the town of Elgin. Such titles as Bless This House, Sleepin' Tinker, This Wasted Day, The Child's Christmas and The Street until, in 1952, she wrote Makar in Miniature, the story of a young girl's life of squalor, street games, gossip and her eventual separation from the mother she adores and her removal to the Orphanage at Skene in Aberdeenshire. A. M. Shinnie, that fine actor whom many Aberdonians will remember from the "old days" of Aberdeen broadcasting, was taking part in "The Makar" and, during rehearsal, said quietly to Jessie, "This is your masterpiece".

Eight years later she developed and transformed "Makar in Miniature" into her book *The White Bird Passes* which has just recently been reprinted by Paul Harris Publishing, and brilliantly dramatised by producer Mike Radford for B.B.C. Television. The work has been recognised as the most moving and poignant comment on those times and has won Jessie Kesson the acclaim she deserves.

Jessie says that her favourite of the Aberdeen productions was her script "And That Unrest" a recollection of a nervous breakdown she herself suffered in her teens for a brief period shortly after leaving the Children's Home. The location is the high walled sanatorium. It's walk time and the inmates must choose from the row of pegs the coats and hats they are to wear. "Mary" chooses hers and starts to giggle. "Here's me stanin' in a lang, wide coat, that lang that it touches the grun. And this big wide hat, so wide that there's nae ordinary shadow o' masel at a'. It's so funny nae hae an ordinary shadow". And at night when the nurse has brought round the sleeping draughts and silence has fallen over the ward there are no more shadows — "except those that flicker in your own mind".

Much of the filming for *The White Bird Passes* was done at Skene Orphanage and on a warm sunny day last year I paid a visit to the Orphanage where Jessie Kesson had spent almost eight years of her life. No more than ten miles west of Aberdeen and not far from the Kirkton of Skene, the house is set amidst farming land in sight and sound of the waters of the Loch of Skene. The granite Victorian Mansion stands in its own grounds approached by a long avenue lined with sycamores and planes and chestnuts. Over the front door is the plaque in memory of the founder

PROCTOR'S
KIRKVILLE ORPHANS HOME
1893

Mr Proctor was a local landowner and benefactor who in his will left what was then a large sum of money to endow the orphanage. The present Matron, Mrs James Mitchell, known as Auntie Wilma to the present day occupants, showed me over the house. There are many modern improvements and Jessie would hardly recognise it now. Where the woodwork used to be dark green and brown there is bright lemon, white and pink. The bedrooms are prettily papered with flowers and the bed-covers are patterned cottons. The kitchen is fitted with new equipment and central heating warms the whole house.

I saw Jessie's one-time dormitory whose sash-windows look onto fields, the laurel hedge and the same tall old sycamores. Daffodils still scatter the earth and the fir tree on the lawn, tousled now with age, carries its huge left-over fir cones for another year. On the hall table lies the Bible presented to the Orphanage in September 1893 "on the occasion of the Opening of the Institution" — the same Bible the children used to read from.

A reception was held in the the B.B.C. Aberdeen and a preview of *The White Bird Passes* shown three days before the actual T.V. transmission and there I met Jessie Kesson again. After twenty years she seemed not to have changed at all. Her beautiful daughter Avril, now in her early forties, is married with a daughter of her own and they live much of the time in their Paris flat in Montmartre. Her son Kenny, whom I remember as a chubby baby on Linksfield Croft, is also married with two daughters. He designs jewellery after an apprenticeship at Hatton Garden.

Untouched by the maturing of life around her and unspoilt by success, Jessie Kesson remains unaffected and natural. On the envelope of the invitation she sent me to attend the reception, she wrote (unsure of my address)

> formerly B.B.C.
> A cottage,
> Aboyne.
> Thank you Postman.

CHAPTER THIRTEEN

George Barron — Gardener Extraordinary

"NO", said George Barron as he dug the new rose-bed in his beautiful little garden at Easdale in the village of Pitmedden near Udny, "Not everyone realises how valuable dung is. Ye must aye hae plenty of muck."

He was planting a couple of dozen rose bushes, the old and new favourites — Piccadilly, Peer Gynt, Silver Jubilee — in the raised border bounded by a wall of granite boulders.

George Barron, now renowned for the expertise and pawky humour which he demonstrates in the BBC T.V. Programme *Beechgrove Garden*, shares the limelight in that popular feature with fellow gardener Jim McColl. His gardening experience goes back many years. As a young man he worked for four years at Monymusk House where his wages were 14 shillings, 16 shillings, then 18 shillings a week. In 1933 he moved on to the Botanic Garden in Old Aberdeen, earning 32s. 6d. a week, out of which he could afford to pay for digs in Merkland Road off King Street. Later he moved to Banffshire, then to the Patons of Grandhome, Potterton and finally, in 1948, to the Great Garden of Pitmedden.

I met him first in 1974 at the Garden of Pitmedden when I was collecting material for *Leopard* magazine for an article on the restoration of that historic garden. He was at that time Head Gardener there and had undertaken the re-creation of the garden under the direction of the late Dr. James Richardson, H.M. Inspector of Ancient Monuments in Scotland.

Sir Alexander Seton, 1st Baronet of Pitmedden, was responsible for the original grand design for the Great Garden in 1675 and it has been said that the laird found inspiration for the formal garden of beautifully laid out parterres, gazebos and fountains from the garden laid out previously at the Palace of Holyroodhouse in Edinburgh for King Charles the First. By the end of the 19th century when the estate passed into the hands of the Keith family the garden had changed its status to that of kitchen garden and orchard. In 1952 Major James Keith CBE, last laird of Pitmedden, presented the mansion and garden to the National Trust for Scotland with an endowment fund to provide for their upkeep. The Trust, in accepting this gift, were determined that the garden should ultimately be restored to its former grandeur, although the destruction by fire of the family papers in 1818 entailed years of research to re-produce a plan of the original geometrical formal garden.

It was at this point that George Barron who had been on the staff since 1948 was entrusted with the practical creation of the garden. As he explained to me as we walked along the terraces, herbaceous borders and tree-lined avenues, it had, at the time of his arrival, been a kitchen garden split up into eight square plots, one of gooseberries, one of peas, one of potatoes and so on.

The parterres are the great achievement. The 3-acre garden is divided into four parterres which are an elaborate arrangement of low-lying flower-beds with paths of turf or gravel between. They contain symmetrical patterns — heraldic emblems, formal and fanciful, outlined with trim borders of box-hedging. Much of the box was obtained from Balmoral and from Haddo House. One parterre represents the coat-of-arms of Sir Alexander Seton flanked by the Scottish saltire and thistle in the appropriate flower-colouring. George Barron told me that all the flowers in the parterres were annuals and every year his wife, from the end of February until the beginning of May, spent each afternoon in the potting shed, pricking out the tiny seedlings into boxes — 35,000 of them for subsequent planting outside.

The garden is cut in two by a grass avenue lined with ten English yew trees each side. They reminded me of the yew trees in the Gardens of the Palace of Versailles. "Yes," he said, "I travelled especially to Versailles to learn from the gardeners there how to trim these particular trees into pyramids, sort of obelisks, on a square base. If you look along the row you'll see they're in a perfect straight line. I used to trim them 'by eye'. Took me a whole day."

At the far end of the yew tree walk a semi-twin stone stairway leads to a magnificent pillared entrance to the upper garden. From the top of this staircase is a panoramic view of the whole scene — the brilliant parterres, the espalier-trained fruit trees clothing the high walls, the rainbow colours of the herbaceous borders planned by the late Lady Burnett of Leys, the ogee-roofed gazebos and the sculptured stone fountain set in the middle of the avenue, surrounded by a pavement of split pebbles, the pebbles having been collected from the River Dee near Banchory.

The revival of the Great Garden of Pitmedden in accordance as far as possible with the designs of the originator Sir Alexander Seton, and now acknowledged as the finest remaining formal garden in Scotland, is a tribute to the enthusiasm of Dr. James Richardson, the foresight of the National Trust for Scotland and above all the horticultural prowess of George Barron.

In 1978 George Barron retired from his post at Pitmedden. A year previously he was awarded the gold medal of the Scottish Horticultural Society for his work at Pitmedden for "outstanding services to Scottish horticulture".

But not for him the life of leisure!

I mentioned the raised border in his small garden at Easdale, supported by great blocks of stone. "There's a story attached to that. I got them from an old out-of-production quarry half a mile from here. It's a hundred feet deep. My wife said, 'If you're going there I'm coming with you.' She tied a rope round my middle and started to let me down over the side. At that moment two girls appeared and looked at us with amazement. One was the daughter of the quarry owner! However they helped me load the stones into the trailer attached to the car. I got them for nothing. Three trailer loads at 6 cwts a time. They make a bonnie wall."

The path at the back of the house was paved with causey blocks. "Three tons from the Council dump at Peterculter — £4 a ton. Near the Rob Roy statue — you keep right along. I picked out the red and white ones."

Many are his activities. He is one of the judges of the best gardens in Aberdeen and miles roundabout for the Britain in Bloom Competition. Along with Jim McColl he recently opened the Pitmedden Garden Centre. Undoubtedly the success of his present career is the Television series *Beechgrove Garden*.

Resting on the granite dyke at Easdale I asked — "How did *Beechgrove Garden* come about?"

"Well, I did two programmes in the *Gardener's World* series with Peter Seabrook at Pitmedden in 1977. At that time the BBC in Aberdeen were thinking of doing a Scottish garden programme and had got in touch with the producer Barry Edgar in Birmingham. Jim McColl had already been asked to take part as co-presenter and Barry Edgar suggested that they went to Pitmedden to have a word with me to see if I was interested in partnering Jim McColl. I'd never met Jim before. We did a pilot programme and I was asked to prepare the garden behind the BBC in Beechgrove Terrace, Aberdeen. For the first two years I looked after the garden, travelling in every morning, but I don't do that now."

There can't be many people in Scotland who haven't viewed *Beechgrove Garden* on BBC 1 (splendidly sub-titled "A weekly digest of gardening advice and information"). In reality the garden is smaller than it appears on camera but it is the prettiest of gardens nestling behind the Engineers' Control Room and you'd never guess that in the centre rises incongruously a 100 feet high television mast, always cleverly avoided by the cameraman.

The original old trees — beech, chestnut, sycamore — inside the walls of the property break the force of the snell wind creeping along Mid Stocket Road. It has everything that a garden should have. Within borders of small flowering shrubs is a fruit and vegetable patch with neat rows of lettuce, runner beans, onions, rasps. Between velvety lawns there are curving paths of sandstone paving slabs, beautifully smooth to enable the producer to get his camera into the right shooting position; a young beech hedge — seven green to one purple — pear trees, apple trees, a little pond with a waterfall, fish and waterlilies; camellias, honeysuckle, greenhouses, grapevines, hanging baskets everywhere, even a model railway. A small area is devoted to a Garden for the Disabled, set about 2 feet high, to encourage gardeners who are in wheelchairs. Open days at the Garden have been an outstanding success and one contribution was a sum of £900 to go to the Fund for the Disabled to buy tools and equipment.

George and Jim make an excellent team and were recently named as top T.V. personalities of the year in Scotland. They are the perfect foil one to the other, lapsing quite naturally into the Doric of their native land — George from Aberdeen, Jim from Kilmarnock.

Unlike many presenters of gardening programmes they do not hesitate to show their disasters as well as their triumphs. Perhaps this is one reason for their popularity.

It's a joy to watch and hear them in the garden — George tasting a sour cherry not yet ripe. "It fairly draws the gums together." Demonstrating a 'press-on stick' to even up the turf, "My own invention — it's called a thumper." Filling his wheelbarrow with

leaf mould, "Jist awa' to the compost heap, autumn is upon us."
Tying chrysanthemums to stakes with soft string not nylon,
"Five lovely stems, five lovely heads." A big green caterpillar on
the palm of his hand, "This lad'll dae a lot of damage — nice
creepie crawlie."

Beechgrove Garden has led to other engagements for George and
Jim, in particular the Road Shows where with a team of two other
experts they answer horticultural questions from the audience and
give advice on the sad, wilting pot-plants proferred to them. Last
summer George was taken ill during the filming of the show at
Broughton in Peebleshire and was rushed to Edinburgh Royal
Infirmary for the removal of a burst appendix.

During his absence two deputies stood in for him in *Beechgrove
Garden* — Douglas MacDonald recently retired Head Gardener at
Crathes Castle and Sandy Rennie, George's near neighbour at
Pitmedden. The invalid's main worry was the progress of his
'tattie barrel' an experiment in the technique of potato growing.

He re-appeared with his colleague Jim McColl a month later.
Now fully recovered he sat by the waterfall cascading into the
flower encircled pond, every corner filled with a cushion of
flowers — bright sea pinks, white helichrysum, miniature blue
phlox. On either side of him sat a pretty young nurse, the two who
had tended him in hospital. He gave them a slice of one of his
cordon-trained Ellison's Orange apples to eat and they munched
appreciatively throughout the programme.

He thanked the viewers for their letters, flowers and good
wishes. "I'm a happy man to have been a gardener all my life."

Chapter 14

People who have gardens

James Hird, council house garden, Summerhill.
Williamina Nicol, Bellenden, Milltimber

> For day's work and week's work
> As I go up and down,
> There are many gardens
> All about the town.
> A kitten and a lilac bush
> Bridal white and tall,
> And later crimson ramblers
> Against a granite wall.

MANY years ago Agnes Mure MacKenzie of Stornoway wrote these words to an air collected on the island of Eigg and called the song "To People Who Have Gardens". The instruction on the music sheet to the singer is "Joyously". And joyously I have no doubt is how the gardeners all about the town of Aberdeen prepare every year for their contribution to the Britain in Bloom Competition organised by the City of Aberdeen Leisure and Recreation Department. Among the team of judges appointed to select the most beautiful gardens was George Barron, late of Pitmedden.

The owners of two gardens I visited have won 1st Prize in their areas consistently for many years. They are Jim Hird who created his little Council House garden about twenty-five years ago at 70 Summerhill Crescent, off King's Gate and Mrs Williamina Nicol who has lived at Bellenden, Milltimber since 1945 and gives all the credit for the beauty of her formal garden to her gardener Peter Kaminskas.

In size Jim Hird's garden doesn't really compare with the 3 acre 17th century Great Garden of Pitmedden, for it is only 20 yards by 9 yards. Yet, in its way, it equally reflects the plans and endeavour of its creator.

Recently retired from Aberdeen Motors, where he was Receiv-
ing Clerk for new cars at the Compound at Portlethen, he can now
spend not only the evening working in the garden but the whole
day long if he wishes. In 1954 he moved into the house when it was
new. "After the builders' rubble was cleared away I planted
potatoes the first year to clean the ground. The second year I cut
out a square border 2 feet all round. I spent my pocket money on
packets of seeds — Sweet William, lupins, Scotch marigolds —
anything to start off a garden. Friends gave me plants. I made the
borders bigger, a curving lawn in the centre. Had the idea of
breaking up a border with an entrance of grass from the path."
    "When did you enter for the Town Council Competition?"
    "For the first time in 1960 and I won a prize of £5. I spent it on
new roses which started my collection."
    What perhaps is most remarkable about this garden is the
profusion of luminous colours. In early September a small rockery
in front of the sitting-room window was smothered with brilliant
blue autumn gentians, dainty pink dianthus with maroon hearts,
miniature blue campanulas, evergreen silvery spikes of the New
Zealand Daisy all interspersed with flowering shrubs — the
carmine red japonica, white and yellow double Scotch roses, a
lovely fuchsia whose buds emerge yellow, then shade to pink
finally to petunia. Under the window a luxuriant purplish clove
hydrangea benefitted from the warmth of the sitting room wall.
    The whole of the front garden can be seen from a stance in the
middle of the lawn surrounded by the borders. The summer had
been dry and some of the herbaceous plants were feeling the effects
of the drought although I could find no fault. Mr Hird said, "The
astilbes have been very unhappy this year. They prefer damp and
shady places. But I don't water the garden. No, no, it's not right to
water."
    The other plants hadn't suffered. He named the sprays of
magenta lythrum salicaria, the white feathery gypsophila, the
woolly foliaged Pearly Everlasting. Most attractive was the Indian
May Apple, flourishing here far from its native Himalayas. In May
the pink flower looks like a closed parasol folded down over its
stalk. But now the red fruits glistened temptingly like sweet
peppers.
    "This is the modern form of orange montbretia — much
stonger. And here's a small pink montbretia."
    Throughout the herbaceous plants were many rose bushes —

floribundas mostly — the gold and apricot Cairngrom, the bright crimson Lilli Marlene, the golden amber Glenfiddich, the vivid vermilion Anne Cocker.

"I love to mix herbaceous with shrubs. I'm not a bedding man. You grow annuals from seed, plant them out, then you throw then away. Not for me! I had to put away the tall delphiniums. There's a difficult wind, a north wind, comes sweeping down the Crescent. The roses don't seem to mind it. My favourite is Silver Jubilee the beautiful peach and cream Hybrid Tea rose. I took a bud off one growing in the front garden and budded it onto a wild rose. I go for a walk in the country and look for a suitable briar in the winter when the sap is down. I'm making it into a standard in the back garden just now. Shall transplant it later."

We walked round the tiny garden again lying between the two paths leading from the road up to the house. Never a weed!

"I think the second flush of roses with their red foliage are at their best in October, colours brighter, fragrance richer. Look at this head of rose buds just waiting to burst into colour. Next month they will look marvellous."

"You don't regret being retired?"

"Oh no! I've got plenty to do. I won't be sitting around."

Aberdeen is divided into different areas for the purposes of the judging and presentation of awards for the superb gardens that lie in the city and round about. Jim Hird's is in the North West area. The garden that won the Silver Shield for the Overall Winner in 1978 is in the Milltimber area on the western outskirts of Aberdeen.

Mrs Nicol entertained me to tea in the upstairs drawing room of the hundred year old granite house. The view from the tall windows is magnificent. Across the Dee valley I could see clearly Kingcausie House in its setting of trees, fields striped with the brilliantly coloured blooms of Anderson's Rose Nursery at Maryculter, and the road winding southwards to Netherley and Stonehaven.

For the more immediate vista between the house and the main Deeside Road — the sweeping lines of orange and red begonias, the velvet lawn, clipped yew trees, weeping standard roses, stone terracing festooned with purple aubretia — Mrs Nicol gave all praise to Peter Kaminskas. His was the basic design meticulously set out on paper shortly after his arrival at Bellenden in 1949. Of Lithuanian nationality, he was a "displaced person" during the last war and spent some years being trained in horticulture at Smith's Nursery at Springhill by whom he was highly recommended to Mrs Nicol.

I asked Peter what the garden was like in those days. "Very different. A long grassy slope running down from the house with clumps of flowers in each corner and some yew trees dotted about."

When we all entered the garden I saw that Peter's design is in the form of a parterre. Picture first a carpet of green — it's hard to call it by such a mundane word as "grass" — fine, short and closely woven. The central feature is a fountain of weathered stone sculptured in the semblance of a woman. The square pond is bounded by a low stone wall surrounded by a crazy paving path. At the four corners are planted quarter beds of richly coloured dwarf begonias. At the furthermost angles of the lawn are four more large quarter beds — floribunda roses, each group an individual hue. Between the rose-beds grow Japanese double pink cherries.

The lawn is backed by three tiers of terraces rising to the level of the house each retaining wall abundantly draped with stone-crops, red and violet aubretias, succulents and dianthus and on each terrace are standard rose trees alternately pink and white.

But what makes this garden such a show piece are the begonias, luminous against the emerald green lawn, ribbons and splashes of colour, circular beds, broad borders, narrow borders, urns, wheelbarrows, window-boxes, all overflowing with this most charming and delicate flower. The begonia, which orginates in Brazil, was brought to Kew Gardens towards the end of last century and has been popular here ever since.

When Peter Kaminskas decided in 1949 to specialise in begonias he bought a few hundred tubers of the variety Multiflora Rex. They have increased by division of the tubers so that he now has four thousand plants. Half are the carmine red "Flamboyant" and half are the apricot-salmon "Madam Richard Galle". The double female flower and the single male flower grow on the same glaucous red stalk rising from a dense cushion of dark green leaves shaped like elongated hearts with purple margins, red-bronze beneath. "They bloom from July till the autumn when I take them up like dahlias when the frost gets them. I keep them all winter in a dry warm bed of sand in the frost free garage. In the middle of February the tubers go into boxes in the greenhouse; in April from greenhouse into frames; in mid June they're planted out in the borders. They flourish in sun or shade."

The drive which is bordered by white and purple lilacs and rhododendrons and some of the original old purple beeches leads past the house to the fruit and vegetable garden behind. As methodically arranged as the flower garden are the lines of lusscious raspberries and strawberries, gooseberries and red currants, potatoes, leeks, peas and carrots. Here too is Peter Kaminskas' cottage where he lives with his Scottish wife Doreen and his two sons. It has its own paved patio, crimson standard roses and red and apricot begonias in wooden tubs. In front of his cottage is a piece of sculpture in the form of three tall crosses of differing heights — the emblem of Lithuania to remind him of home.

I asked him if he'd any hobbies. He opened the door of his bungalow. Lining the walls of the hall were rows and rows of small square frames and in each frame stood a miniature unopened bottle of liqueur. Hundreds of them! Some were porcelain, some were glass. Cherry Brandy in the Eiffel Tower. Apricot liqueur in a water-carrier figurine, Curaçao in a Chinese Mandarin, the Spirit of Scotland (whisky) in a book like a bible. They come from Holland, Malta, Italy, the Highlands.

"My wife and I have collected them for thirty years — and we're both teetotalers!"

He confided to me, "I've no outside interests. The garden is the love of my life". Mrs Nicol confided to me with a twinkle in her eye, "I'm not allowed to touch anything, only to look. I have to sneak out at dead of night if I want to pick a flower!"

As we all three walked along the spectacular beds of begonias which were intermixed with "dot plants" — fuchsia, antirrhinum and geranium — a long distance coach of holiday makers drew up outside the gate. All the passengers stood up in their seats and peered delightedly over the beech hedge.

> For day's work and week's work
> As I go up and down,
> There are many gardens
> All about the town.
> I have passed your railings,
> When you never knew,
> And people who have gardens
> I give my thanks to you.

Chapter 15

Bessie Brown,
Teacher of Piping

Snow at Aboyne.
Slush at Kincardine O'Neil.
Rain at Banchory.

THAT'S usually the way of it in February, the opening month of
the salmon fishing on the Aberdeenshire Dee. Who better to
go and see than Bessie Brown who lives at Heatherdale Cottage off
the Raemoir Road at Banchory. She is an expert and famous
throughout Scotland, England and abroad for the tying of exquisite salmon flies and counts Royalty among her many customers. The skies were grey and full of moisture, the bare birch
branches dripping icy globules into the pools of sodden sand used
to grit the treacherous roads. A cock pheasant flew into a tall pine
tree uttering its insistent call as I approached the cottage with its
bright red framed windows. The door to the kitchen was open and
Bessie in her wheelchair was washing the dishes after lunch. A
good coal fire in the sitting-room banished the February gloom
outside. Everywhere there were books, on tables, settee, piano-
top, chairs, even the floor, and papers, music manuscripts, chan-
ters — the friendly clutter of a room whose owner is independent,
content and immersed in her work.

It's at least thirty-five years since I recorded Bessie Brown in an
interview for the Overseas Service of The B.B.C. I took a portable
recorder to her cottage beside the River Dee on the Blackhall
Estate near Banchory. Since 1910 she had shared a home with her
sister Violet, her brother Robert, Pipe Major at Balmoral, and her
father Frank Brown, head game-keeper on the Estate which at
that time belonged to James T. Hay. The Blackhall cottage was on
the south side of the river where the salmon fishermen stand thigh
deep in their rubber waders. She'd been at school just six weeks
when she contracted polio at the age of six years. There was no

cure at that time and she has conducted her life ever since from the confines of a wheel chair. Accompanied by the sounds of willow-warblers and yellow-hammers, within sight of the flock of swans on the river come down from the Loch of Aboyne she described in the recording the "Jeannie" fly-black with the creamy-white feathers of the jungle-cock, the golden and red "Logie", and "Blue Charm", the delicate feathers, the tinsels, silks and floss, the feathers of Widgeon and Mallard duck and crest of Golden Pheasant.

In 1954 the family moved to Heatherdale the little cottage built, by coincidence, by my one-time neighbour Mrs Squair when I lived in Forest Avenue, Aberdeen. Now Bessie lives there alone, her father having died in 1955 after he'd been there for just one year. Her sister Violet died from influenza in 1962. And her brother Bob, the Queen's Piper, who spent forty years at Balmoral as game-keeper and ghillie during the day and played the pipes while guests dined at the castle every evening, died in 1972.

Over tea and Scotch shortbread we talked of the old days of the pipers as that same cock pheasant flew past the window.

"That's Johnnie my pheasant. Roosts in my trees. He's been here four years. I feed him on bread and dry porridge oats. He has six plump hens who seem to live in the garden too."

"Aren't you frightened he'll be shot?"

"A party came shooting just beyond the garden and I said 'Don't shoot my alarm clock' and so far they haven't."

"The tradition is that the Pipe Major plays at every dinner at Balmoral?"

"Yes. George V was a great man for the pipes. Brother Bob started learning at ten years on the chanter. His teachers were famous in their day — Wiliam Fraser, Jonathan Ewing and P.M. Ewing. He won Pibroch prizes at Oban, then with Bob Nicol of Durris. King George was so impressed with their playing that he sent them both to Pipe Major John McDonald of Inverness for six weeks to have their playing perfected. Bob won prizes all over the place — twelve times winner in London of the Gillies Cup for Pibroch. Pibrochs are lovely — sad tunes and glad tunes, all different."

"Have you a favourite tune?"

"Perhaps 'The Children's Lament'. The man who composed it had lost his seven children. Or maybe 'Lament for Patrick Ogg McCrimmon'. The composer heard that McCrimmon had died.

He wrote his Lament, then heard that he was alive after all and presented the tune to him."

"Do you compose?"

"Oh I've no ability for that. Whenever I tried it, I found it was like someone else's tune! All my family were champion pipers in this district. My three uncles were excellent."

"And your father?"

"Not a piper my father. He was Frank Brown a native of Finzean, one of the family of Browns who worked the Bucket Mill. My grandfather was the man who in 1853 started the Bucket Mill in the Forest of Birse — Peter Brown a mill-wright. The last of the Browns, Willie Brown, died ten years ago and since then the place has become derelict though the special antique machinery has gone to the Museum of Antiquities of Scotland."

"I remember buying a bucket there, the traditional 'bowie', a small bucket of wooden staves and metal hoops. I still use it to put pot plants in."

"People used to come from far and near to buy a hand-made wooden bucket. They lasted a life-time. When plastic took over from wood it spelt the end of the Bucket Mill. It was one of only three mills in the Feugh Valley powered by water. There was a meal mill now out of use and a turning mill which does still work. There's word the Bucket Mill is going to be restored with help from the landowner Mr Angus Farquharson, though it'll cost about £12,000 to bring it back to working order."

"When did you start to teach bagpipe playing?"

"At the end of the last war the late Sir James Burnett of Leys asked me to learn Army Cadets at the Banchory Drill Hall. There's an awful lot of young players. Many want to learn. Years ago children used to walk three mile to have a tune with me. But now fathers and mothers deliver the children by car and leave them for only twenty minutes!"

"Which are best — boys or girls?"

"Girl pupils are very quick to take up. They practise and practise till they get it right. Boys have so many distractions. Biggest trouble is T.V.

My best player is from Aboyne, Edward Smith, eight years old, son of the Water Inspector at Aboyne. He plays a miniature set of pipes. A little star in the making. His brother Ian is a prize-winner too. And I've a good girl piper at Kingswells."

"They start on a practice chanter?"

"Aye, before the pipes. It costs around £10 now, a full sized one £20. First I teach them to put their fingers on the chanter correctly. Then I learn them the scale. Learn them from D to E transition, not falsely, careful, then on to doublin' — that's grace notes. Give them a simple tune. Put three fingers down, keep little finger up. I know the difference if incorrect fingering. They say 'But you're not looking at me'. Don't need to. I can hear. I sing the tune to them to give expression."

Her chanter was lying on the table.

"That was a Christmas present from my father — a Peter Henderson model over sixty years old. I value that chanter a lot."

"Play me tune."

"There's lots of lovely times. I'll play you 'Dark Island'. It's a slow air that comes from the Highlands perhaps."

Cheeks blown out, she played the pure sad notes filling the cottage and the heather garden.

"There was a slow air competition seven years ago at Turriff. I learnt a young lad that tune and he won 1st Prize. Now he's got married. Ach, they get married and the pipes get shoved in below the bed."

"You always attend the Highland Games?"

"I can't make up my mind which I like best — Aboyne or Lonach. I've been every year at Aboyne since 1920. What a record! I judge the local competitions at Lonach, though it can be starving cold there. I love the March of the Clansmen — a hundred men and boys — the greatest spectacle in Scotland."

"Do you keep any pet animals?"

"My neighbour's cat goes through to my bed sometimes to have a nap. I love my wild birds — the robins, great tits, pigeons, jackdaws, crows, a sparrow-hawk. There was a Greater Spotted Woodpecker, parents and three young down the road. Before the pine trees grew up there used to be hundres of yellow yities and warblers. There was a mole-hill in the garden with a hole in it. I watched it and 'His Majesty Moley' peered out of the hole. 'What are ye dein there?' He quickly popped back."

"You couldn't poison them?"

"I could not. I *hate* mole-catchers. When we was children we was terrified of a mole-catcher we called 'Moley Brodie'. The story was that if he shook your hand, ye'd never see yer hand again."

"Do you still tie fishing flies?"

"Only if I'm asked to. I've never fished in my life but I can dress a fly to catch a fish. I don't wear glasses though. I still believe in my own eyes at seventy-eight."

"Do you have a home-help?"

Her eyes laughed. "No. I was offered Meals on Wheels. I replied — 'I'm on the wheels, but do my own meals'."

As I was leaving a girl pupil of nine years came for her lesson, bringing her own chanter. I walked round the garden, shrouded in mist, scattering the hen pheasants among the heather to the music perhaps of another prize-winner.

Bessie Brown, whose greatest pleasure in life is teaching children to play the bagpipes, has just been awarded the British Empire Medal for her services to piping — her teaching and judging at the many Highland Gatherings throughout the country.

Chapter 16

Walter Leiper, Lapidarist

ALL over the world there exist jewels which are still embedded in the rock in which they were formed millions of years ago. Where are they to be found in the north-east — these semi-precious stones?

The whisky-coloured quartz, the cairngorm, comes from the Cairngorm Mountains, the eastern cliffs of Beinn à Bhuird, Culblean Hill and the Pass of Ballater; red garnets are found in granite and mica-schists in Glen Ey, Glen Callater and Pannanich; the blue topaz at the water-shed of the River Dee; tourmaline and beryl in the granite quarry at Rubislaw; Scotch pearls in the quiet stretches of the river at Banchory, Cambus o' May and Aboyne.

A specialist in the field of cutting and polishing some of these stones is Walter Leiper of Garlogie. Fourteen years ago the solid granite school and adjoining school-house on the south side of the Garlogie Road about ten miles from Aberdeen became available and were rented by Mr Leiper. The children now go to school at Echt and Skene.

One time climber and collector of gem-stones he uses the largest classroom of the former school as his workshop and showroom, the walls still panelled with their original tongued and grooved boarding but desks and seats removed. The wide windows look to the south over his work-bench. He lives next door in the school-house with this wife.

He was at work at the grinding machine when I entered — fiftyish, robust, silver-haired, clad in a dark grey dust coat. The whole room was sparkling with the lights reflected from the facets of the semi-precious stones, like an Aladdin's cave of treasures. Ranged on the shelves along the walls were large specimens of rock crystal from Deeside, pale amethyst from Siberia, slices of agate from Montrose, a hollow geode cut in two, the cavity lined with tiny purple crystals. In glass cases were his finished products — pendants, ear-rings, finger-rings, brooches set with cairngorms, rose-quartz, amethyst; agate-based pen-holders, letter-openers, knives with Iona marble handles — examples of the skill and artistry of this traditional craftsman.

He was cutting a slab of agate on the machine into workable slices. Then he laid a metal template pattern on a slice of agate and with an aluminium pencil marked out the shape for the pendant. Next he cut the stone with the diamond-toothed wheel over which water dripped continuously. Then grinding, sanding and grinding again to make ready for polishing on leather with tin oxide.

I asked him what started his interest in gem cutting and polishing.

"As a child of about ten I took a book out of the library *Gems of Scotland* by McCulliam. That led me to Dr Heddle's famous book *The Mineralogy of Scotland* and this really stimulated my interest. Then I went out on a mineral collecting expedition and discovered my first crystals. It was a great thrill — on Kincorth Hill south of Aberdeen long before any houses were built. There used to be quarries. On the hillsides of Kincorth there were veins of quartz. I expect they're still knocking around somewhere.

"Did you take up lapidary at an early age?"

"I tried a business career at first, as agent for a manufacturer of electric blankets and pharmaceuticals. I thought — why sell other people's goods? — decided to sell my own. I started first of all at Cults for two years then came to Garlogie."

"Is the equipment expensive?"

"Yes — though you only buy once. But replacements of parts are continuous. The steel circular blades I use for cutting every kind of stone are impregnated with diamond along the edge. They have little notches of diamonds and need regular renewal once a year."

He showed me boxes of rough stones that he works.

"In the raw state minerals are more beautiful than man could design. For instance this cluster of purple fluorspar cubes — every mineral has a characteristic shape. Single crystals of fluorspar are perfect cubes. Sometimes the cubes like these join together and form twins of bluish green. I used to find quite a lot of crystals on Geallaig Hill."

"I've heard that fluorspar, when it's washed, smells like the earth."

"Yes that earthy smell seems like a link between us and the earth the stones were born in millions of years ago. Fluorspar is a fascinating mineral. If you shine an ultra-violet lamp on the crystals contained in a black box they glow. It's known as the black light — a tremendous thing."

"Do you still search for stones yourself?"

"Not so much now. I let it be known that I'm in the market for stones. Climbers, students often, come to show me what they've found. They know the clefts in the rocks to search. I buy from them. That defrays their weekend expenses! A favourite hunting-ground is the granite top of the mountain Beinn à Bhuird north of Braemar, particularly for cairngorms."

"Do you know the story of the old lady who found an enormous cairngorm on Beinn à Bhuird?"

"Her name was A'Chailleach nan Clach and she found it 200 years ago, 4,000 feet up the mountain and presented it to the Laird of Invercauld. She must have been a tough old lady. She carried it ten miles to Invercauld Castle and it weighed over 50 lbs. That cairngorm is a blackish brown, 2 feet long and like all quartz it has the characteristic shape — a hexagonal prism with pyramid top. I've seen it on show at Braemar Castle where there is a fine collection of stones in their raw state, collected by Captain Alwyne Farqurharson of Invercauld.

The biggest stone I've ever cut was a cairngorm. So seldom you find a crystal which will yield one large single stone. It was 294 carats, a pinkish smoky tinge. It was 100% Scottish!

Another of my cairngorms, a light amber colour, is at St James Palace. Set in a rose bowl it was presented by Aberdeen City to Princess Anne on her marriage."

A large tray of pebbles all shapes and sizes, clear, cloudy, variegated, lay on a table. "Do you have what's called a pebble-tumbler for polishing?"

"Not a tumbler but an electric vibrator. I put in small pebbles collected from river-bed or sea-shore and add water and grit. After a few days vibrating they're smooth and glistening."

"Do you sell them as they are?"

"Yes, or I mount them in silver to turn them into brooches and pendants."

I picked up from his bench a lump of lovely blue stone flecked with what looked like gold dust.

"That's lapis lazuli — not Scottish. Afghanistan is its home. I got it from an Edinburgh monumental granite polishing company when they went out of business recently. They had been commissined to make a St Andrew's Cross, the lapis lazuli forming the background to the cross and I got the surplus. I've already made some pendants from it. The tiny fragments of sparkling gold are sulphide of iron, better known as iron pyrites. You can't combine it with silver as it blackens silver."

Mr Leiper showed me his note-book where he had recorded where his stones came from.

A yellow opaque beryl from Rubislaw Quarries.
Black Tourmalines from Glen Clova, Kildrummy, Rubislaw.
Cairngorms from the steep face of the Pass of Ballater and from the bed of the River Avon near Tomintoul.
Pinkish quartz from Brindy Hill near Premnay.
Scarlet quartz (stained by iron) from the west shoulder of Mount Keen.

"When Rubislaw was a working quarry the beautiful crystals that were found in the quarry were kept in the shed at the top. It was like a little museum.

People can easily be fooled by the colours of crystals — stained by vegetation. They're not necessarily the same colour inside as outside."

From another box Mr Leiper took out some distorted mussel shells and the oddly shaped small Scotch pearls which he had extracted from them.

"These are fresh water mussels. I found them in the River Dee near the archeological dig at Crathes Bridge. You can guess which are the mussels containing pearls. The shells are always lumpy."

They were all different sizes and shapes and colours — pink, purple, copper, deep cream, lilac, pure white.

"How do they come in so many shades?"

"The colour is controlled by the state of health of the mussel!"

"Do you have any difficult customers?"

He smiled. "Some years ago an Aberdeen solicitor came to see me and produced from his pocket a superb piece of Chinese jade with beautiful configurations. He asked me to cut it down the middle, explaining that a woman had left a will stipulating that all her possessions were to be divided equally between two beneficiaries!"

In addition to accepting commissions to design, make and repair jewellery Mr Leiper has now diversified into glass engraving. His craftsmanship is of the greatest delicacy. Using an old dental drill — foot controlled — he engraves his drawings free hand. Upon a stand in front of the window were six slender-stemmed wine glasses each engraved with a bird that breeds in Scotland. The sunshine playing on the glass outlined feather and wing. My favourite was the Arctic tern drifting over its native marsh-land.

St Machar's Cathedral and King's College were two of the subjects on the wine carafes, and castles of the north-east were engraved on a set of whisky glasses. A placard on the wall with photographs and sketches of the castles gave a brief history of each and is of great interest to visitors from overseas.

"Do you sell your glasses abroad?"

"I recently sent a set of six whisky glasses on a trade mission to Texas inaugurated by British Caledonian Airways. Several orders were the result."

Be it designing, cutting and polishing, engraving, here is a craftsman who finds tremendous satisfaction in upholding the traditions of skill in the north-east.

Chapter 17

Harold Esslemont — In an Alpine Garden

SOME people ascend mountains for the joy and satisfaction of discovering gem-stones among the rocks. Others, equally enthusiastic, derive their pleasure from finding Alpine plants growing in the rock crevices or breaking their way through the crumbling crust of snow.

In the city of Aberdeen lives a well-known businessman who is also a world-renowned authority on Alpine plant cultivation. He is Harold Esslemont who recently celebrated his 80th birthday and announced his retirement as Chairman of the exclusive Department Store, Messrs. Esslemont and Macintosh, after sixty-two years with the company. He said he thought it was time to hand over to a younger man although he will still be a director. His age is difficult to believe when one sees the youthful figure walking smartly down Albyn Place in summer time in light grey coat with light grey bowler to match.

When I met him recently at his home in Forest Road he told me of some of the tours he had enjoyed and which were organised by the Alpine Garden Society. They went to the Dolomites, Greece, Rhodes, Switzerland, Italy, Turkey and were led by guides who were themselves experts. A specialist from Wisley Gardens took them through the Lebanon from the heat of Beirut to the snow-clad slopes of Mount Lebanon where the magnificent and ancient cedars still thrive. In the Peloponnese they saw whole fields of fragrant wild pink cyclamen and in Turkey fritillaries grew plentifully in spite of the wandering goats.

I asked, "Where should the novice plant-hunter start looking?"

"I'd recommend a visit to Pontresina in Switzerland in spring. A great advantage is the number of ski-lifts which can be used not only be skiers. They're good things especially for the not so young.

You can ascend by the lifts, swaying gently over the flower-strewn meadows and then walk down searching for your plants on the way — the violet blue soldanella, woolly edelweiss, gentians, anemones."

"Are you allowed to take living plants?"

"It is sometimes possible to collect a few plants, but an import licence is required to bring them into Britain. In some countries the removal of rare plants however is forbidden and plant wardens keep a sharp lookout for the covetous!"

We passed from the house by a glazed door into the small back garden.

"Before I specialised in Alpines I planted as you can see a north facing peat border for azaleas, meconopsis, primulas and the tall orange Japanese lily called Hansonii."

In the shelter of a paved patio a camellia bush was trained against one wall, already in bud at the end of March which was unusually early for the north east. These hardy Williamsii varieties have come through the recent severe winter unscathed.

Mr Esslemont conducted me down the garden to the alpine house concealed behind a trellis.

"This was built to my own specification in 1960. I spend two or three hours here most mornings. It has no heating though I am not dogmatic about this. But I do believe that alpines which will tolerate frost retain their character better in a cold house. There is full top and side ventilation and slatted sun-blinds. You'll see that the plants are in clay pots or pans which are plunged in a bed of sand. This reduces the need for constant watering. Since birds could fly through the open windows and plunder the blossom I protect the precious pans with netting. Five years' work could be lost in five minutes."

The sand plunge bed, on a three feet high staging, was as neat and precise as I had expected from a perfectionist like Mr Esslemont. Nearly all the plants were in the shape of fat rounded cushions, compact and firm. One of the most beautiful cushions was a rare species called Primula allionii. A profusion of short-stemmed crimson flowers almost concealed the tightly compressed mat of rosettes of small grey-green leaves.

"It originates in the Maritime Alps, inhabiting cracks in the rocks, always with a northern exposure. Here I grow it in a compost containing one-third lime chips and I re-pot it every third year. I obtained my specimen many years ago from a collection which was being dispersed. It's long-living, already thirty years old!"

"Do you grow from seed?"

"Well, take this Swiss Androsace or Rock Jasmine."

I looked at another cushion plant, the woolly leaves covered with tiny white flowers.

"I've seen this growing in rock crevices on the Weisshorn at 6,000 feet, well above the timber line. The best method of propagation is by seed rather than by cuttings. I sow my seeds in December and expose them to wintry conditions, covering them with snow when it is available. When the seedlings are large enough I pot them up in thumbs and when they flower for the first time I select a few of the best forms to grow on and I discard the others. A collar of hard tufa limestone rock built around the plant makes a firm base for the cushion and helps to protect the vulnerable neck. Cushions are usually at their best for exhibition from six to eight years old."

"Have you any special advice to give regarding the cultivation of the Androsace?"

"Yes — three don'ts! Don't over-pot, don't over-water and don't encourage aphis."

Many interesting plants come from further afield, from countries that few can afford the time and money to visit. Expeditions are organised to Iran, Afghanistan, Nepal and the Andes bringing back a wealth of material — plants, bulbs and seeds which the cultivator at home can purchase to extend his personal collection. Mr Esslemont calls this "plant-hunting by proxy".

One "by proxy plant" in the alpine house was the fritillary belonging to the lily family which came from Iran. The variety I liked was the Fritillaria michaelovskii its blossom shaped like a Victorian hanging lampshade, coloured bronze with a yellow edge and six little brown dots inside the petals. Other combinations of colour were orange and scarlet or green and purple in a pattern of squares which gave it its alternative name of Checker-lily. "It is increasing well from the original single bulb," I was told, "and in time it could be an interesting pan."

Another most "interesting pan" contained a mound of diminutive yellow flowers — Dionysias aretioides — a plant that grows in the cracks of limestone cliffs in Iran near the Caspian Sea.

"I like to grow the more difficult plants, particularly species of Dionysias, often in double pots to permit more accurate watering.

They can be propagated by cuttings although most of my plants are grown from detritus."

"Detritus?"

"Brushings from live plants in nature sent me by collector friends often contain seeds. I spread the detritus over the soil in plastic trays in December, cover it with a thin layer of fine gravel and leave the trays in a cold north frame where they will get well frosted. Seedlings germinate in April or May."

"If I tried to grow Dionysias from seed how long before it flowered?"

"Oh not long — about nine years."

One of the strangest plants of which he has a specimen is Raoulia eximia. They grow in tussocks on the screes and rocky outcrops of the slopes of Mount Edward in New Zealand. They look like recumbent sheep, the woolly rosettes of creamy buff resembling the tight curls of a sheep's fleece. The other name is Vegetable Sheep.

"To keep them happy you must remember that they endure snow, rain and cold. I keep them moist, shaded in summer, and on warm evenings give them a light spray to remind them of their mountain home. It's so important to understand the nature of one's plants."

That seems to be the crux of the matter — the understanding of the individual alpines.

Mr Esslemont has a tremendous record of prize winning and his exhibits of rare plants may be seen every year at the end of May at the Flower Show organised by the Aberdeen Branch of the Scottish Rock Garden Club in the Ballroom of the Music Hall in Aberdeen.

As a prominent member of this Club he was invited in 1974 to give the William Buchanan Memorial Lecture in Edinburgh on "Some aspects of Alpine Cultivation". He ended his erudite lecture with a quotation from a fellow expert: "It takes two lifetimes to grow alpines — the first to gain experience, the second to cultivate them".

Chapter 18

H Adair Nelson
The Early Days of His
Majesty's Theatre

ON my writing desk lie a pile of Theatrical Tour Cards dated
from 1901, a police whistle and a silver topped Malacca cane,
a few souvenirs of my father's life in the theatre.

My father Harry Adair Nelson came from Bath and at the turn
of the century had run and owned, in conjunction with his
brother, the little pantomime theatre The Prince of Wales in
Liverpool. On the death of Queen Victoria in 1901 his theatre, to
his great financial loss, was forced to close down. Shortly afterwards he became No. 1 Touring Manager for the famous George
Edwardes Company. I see from the company's tour cards that in
the year 1906 he was in charge of the Spring Tour of the musical
comedy *The Little Michus* visiting cities in the north of England,
Dublin, Glasgow and Edinburgh. Unexpectedly he was offered by
Robert Arthur, the London impressario, the management of a
new theatre that was being built in Aberdeen. A year previously he
had married Florence Hounsell from Bristol and the acceptance of
this offer gave him the opportunity in the autumn of 1906 to settle
down in Aberdeen which he referred to as "this enchanting place".

The earlier playhouse Her Majesty's Theatre in Guild Street
(later re-named The Tivoli) had served the public since 1872 and
was owned by Robert Arthur in addition to a similar theatre in
Dundee and a chain of theatres in England. With his decision to
build His Majesty's Theatre was linked the realisation that the city
of Aberdeen, rapidly developing and spreading into the surrounding green fields, required and deserved the very best that touring
companies could give.

So at a cost of £35,000 he built His Majesty's on what must at
first have seemed an inappropriate site for a theatre — on Rose-

mount Viaduct above the deep valley through which ran the stream called the Denburn. In fact it turned out to be the best site possible — at the apex of a triangle which widened out into the sunken flowered and wooded gardens of Union Terrace, over-looked by the sweep of the grand granite buildings — banks, insurance companies and Council offices which were rising along the west side of the terrace. The elevated position of the site ensured that all the front entrances to the theatre could be at the level of the Viaduct while the stage door was set deep in the hollow of the valley.

The architect was an Englishman Frank Matcham whose de-sign, with its pillared Grecian frontage, arched windows and glowing copper dome, set a standard that has seldom been surpas-sed anywhere in the country.

Perhaps the finest view of His Majesty's Theatre is from Union Bridge, part of the Union Street fly-over, that great engineering feat designed and built in the early 19th century. Between the decorative leopards, heraldic beasts of the city, erected on the north side of the metal ornamental balustrade of the bridge you can glimpse this most magnificent theatre, its white facade of Kemnay granite sparkling even on the dullest day.

The railway line from Aberdeen to the North of Scotland ran alongside the Gardens and trains stopped at a small station called "Schoolhill", literally a few yards from the rear of the theatre. With great convenience scenery, props and costume baskets could be transferred almost direct from the goods train to the low level storage area.

In the photograph of the theatre (taken about 1906) the little railway station, long since demolished, can be seen over the Viaduct.

The Opening date, after several years of planning and building, was fixed for Monday 3rd December 1906.

Four days before the Opening Night, on November 29th, the City Magistrates paid a formal visit to the theatre to inspect and approve the interior furnishings and equipment. According to the *Evening Gazette* of that date, "They were highly pleased with the progress of the work which was in a very advanced state of completion. The contractors for the seating accommodation are now well within the realisation of their task." In fact the tradesmen realised their task by working overtime every evening and the deadline was met!

The great day arrived and Aberdeen had never seen anything quite like it. Every reserved seat in the house had been booked for weeks in advance, and by 5 o'clock crowds began to queue for the early doors. Not only was there a large body of policemen in attendance but Chief Constable William Anderson himself was present to control the crowds, as one horse-drawn carriage after another rolled up to the brilliantly lit entrance.

The foyer, floored with black and white chequered marble, was crowded with Town and Gown and County, the gentlemen in white tie and tails accompanied by their ladies in full evening dress and jewels. Also in evening dress my father greeted the guests.

The names of the original staff are still remembered. Brown, the doorman, who came forward to open the doors of carriage or cab; Benzie just inside the vestibule who collected the tickets; Miss Peters who presided in the Dress Circle Bar; Miss Moir who sold the programmes, Webberley, the Head Electrician, Johnnie Small the Scenery Painter, Waldie, the Carpenter.

The first production was the operatic pantomime *Little Red Riding Hood* which ran to packed houses for four weeks. The *Gazette* advertised it as "Having special scenery, new and elaborate costumes, a chorus of forty trained voices, children's ballet and the Poppyland Troupe Dancers." The name part was played by Nellie Wigley who sang "I wouldn't leave my Little Wooden Hut for you." Although the opening performance was not of a high cultural quality the audience was delighted. The auditorium at that time seated 2,550 and not only was every seat occupied but people were sitting on the steps of the dress circle as well.

Apart from an Edinburgh firm which was responsible for supplying the draperies and furnishings, the craftsmanship was entirely that of Aberdeen firms — masons, plasterers, joiners, painters, plumbers, slaters, electricians and upholsterers. How beautiful it must have looked. The illumination was scintillating, the white ceiling encrusted with crystal chandelier drops. The decorative plaster work, carried out by James Scott and Son, formed a frieze above the proscenium arch and life-sized figures over the upper boxes, designed by W. Hamilton Buchan of Union Row, represented the Goddesses of Tragedy and Comedy. No pillars interrupted the view as the cantilever system of support for the balconies had been adopted. Throughout the theatre the upholstery was crimson — the velvet seats, carpets and curtains at the four boxes. Beneath the splendid marble proscenium was

draped a rich crimson cloth bearing a gilt crown with the Royal
Monogram at either side.

The newspaper critics gave full rein to their powers of praise,
reporting that "There is much that will appeal to the children in
Red Riding Hood. There is plenty of clean harmless mirth, but
there is an even higher appeal in the artistic beauty of the
production. It is a pantomime of good taste and irreproachable
morale, an entertainment that all may see with profit and pleasure."

On entering the theatre each member of the audience was
presented with a booklet, now of historical value, entitled "The
Playhouse of Bon-Accord — Being a short survey of the actor's art
in the City of Aberdeen from forgotten times to the erection of His
Majesty's Theatre by Mr Robert Arthur in Rosemount Viaduct."
The text ended with the words, "Now it remains with the people of
Aberdeen to put the copestone of success on what the craftsmen of
Aberdeen have builded with so much care." I still have my
parents' copy.

As children my sister Peggy, my two brothers Bill and Hal and I
lived with our parents at 65 Osborne Place at the corner of Prince
Arthur Street. The house is now a Nursery School. A few houses
further down lived an elderly lady named Mrs Shaw. She was a
phrenologist. I don't know if it was the sight of her dark face
peering through the curtains or the placard hanging in the front
window portraying a life-sized head divided up into its cranial
sections that scared us most!

We passed a very happy childhood. As salaries go nowadays we
were anything but rich but money went a long way. On an income
of £400 per annum we were able, in the early twenties, to live very
comforably. School fees at the High School and the Grammar were
£3 a term, the rent of a large house £60 a year, best fillets of
haddock from Alexanders at Holburn Junction 1/6 a lb., a tram-
ride to the Sea Beach one penny.

We had a large flower filled garden at the back — Montbretia,
tiger lilies, pinks, London Pride, bluebells and small red rambling
roses up the walls. There were four trees at the end sycamores and
horse chestnuts each appropriated by one child according to
height. Every summer evening at 6 o'clock before he left for the
theatre my father would walk round the garden and I was deputed
to choose a small carnation for his buttonhole. He would catch the
tram at the junction of Albyn Place and Prince Arthur Street as far

as Union Terrace. Few people had cars in these days.

Shortish in height, strongly built, he was always impeccably dressed. His suits were tailored at W.J. Milne's (opposite the Northern Club that was). His lace up boots of softest leather were perfection, specially made for him by Dunns at the same time as the accompanying 3-piece boot-trees. He wore white starched wing collars and bow tie with his soft white shirts and across his waistcoat hung his gold watch-chain with a silver watch tucked into one pocket and a silver wax Vesta match case in the other pocket. He always brushed the nap of his bowler hat with a velvet pad before putting it on. In his right hand was a silver topped cane. I remember one cane especially which had a silver French franc set into the top. My brother Bill remembers that another of his canes was a sword stick — for defence against possible muggers who existed then as they do today. My favourite, which I still have, was a Malacca cane with silver top and deer horn ferrule, presented to him by his friend the famous actor Fred Terry on a visit to Aberdeen in 1918.

My father considered His Majesty's Theatre to be "his theatre" for every moment of his personal management during the first seventeen years and he felt than an essential part of our education was to attend the theatre nearly every week.

Pantomimes then as now were the great attraction at Christmas time and we passed the afternoon of Christmas Eve impatiently at our various pursuits until it was time to leave home. I remember it so clearly — my sister Peggy humming Plaisir d'Amour as she put the finishing touches to her pencil sketch of the corridors of the Aberdeen High School for Girls (she subsequently became an accomplished artist); my brother Bill swotting German verbs in his bedroom; my younger brother Hal chuffing round the sitting-room on an upturned chair pretending he was a railway train; I making silhouette shadows on the wall for my jet black kitten Kiki to leap at.

By the time that Leerie came to light the street gas lamp at our corner, about half past three, my mother would have unstrapped her old theatrical travelling basket and laid out on the table the signed photographs of her favourite actors and actresses of the 1890's. She told us stories of Mabel Love, Edward Compton (father of Fay Compton and Compton Mackenzie), Martin Harvey, Ellen Terry, Jessica Thorne, Lawrence Irving, Eugene Stratton. The display culminated with a group photograph of the entire company of the musical production *The Lady Slavey* of which she herself had been a member in 1901.

Be the pantomime Mother Goose, Cinderella, Dick Whittington the excitement was the same. We sat in the 'Manager's Box'. I usually in the alcove known as the 'cubby-hole'. Before the curtain rose the magical moment of expectation while the orchestra was tuning up. The wonder of the transformation scenes where with just a change of lighting and the raising of a gauze veil the stage was transformed from a work-a-day kitchen into a glittering ballroom.

One of my pleasures, during the orchestral overture, was to study the drop curtain separating audience from stage. I was fascinated by the larger than life painting on the pale golden curtain of a pastoral scene of groups of figures talking and laughing against a background of woodland trees and sculptured terraces. In the foreground two dancing partners in early 18th century shimmering silken costumes bowed and curtsied in a stately dance. Below the picture were the words The Minuet. I had for years wondered what this picture was, and a recent visit to the Aberdeen Reference Library has revealed that this scene must have been based on the oil-painting by the French artist Watteau entitled *Les Fêtes Venitiennes*. The Theatre had always fascinated Watteau and the subject of his original painting was probably suggested by the Minuet Intermezzo in the ballet Les Fêtes Venitiennes performed at the Paris Opera in 1710. Who was responsible for painting the curtain I haven't been able to ascertain. It was replaced by a sumptuous red velvet curtain to match the proscenium hangings about 1955 which to me was a disappointment.

Sometimes I would look up from the box to see my father standing on the little balustraded balcony to the right of the dress circle leading to the stairs to his office, surveying the audience like a captain from his bridge. I have even seen him take his white handkerchief and wipe imaginary flecks of dust from the handrail.

In the intervals we nibbled Nestlé's milk chocolate medallions from a red and gold cylindrical packet. After the final curtain the audience had barely filed through the exits when the ushers began to lay the long dust-sheets over the rows of seats in the stalls.

Early one Christmas morning my father and mother silently carried into our room a specially made wooden model of His Majesty's Theatre about 3 feet high by 2 feet deep, with raked stage, proscenium arch, orchestra pit, wings and flies, velvet drop curtain and drapes. The actors were cardboard cut-outs in Shakespearean costume. Electricity by means of batteries was installed in footlights and spotlights by Mr Webberley the theatre electrician and the scenery was realistically painted by Mr Small. We had years of pleasure making up our own plays.

Although my father was immensely popular and one of the kindest men he was a strict disciplinarian both at home and in the theatre. My mother used to say that he was obsessed by the moral and material perfection of the theatre in his charge. So you can imagine what he felt on a "Students' Night", a feature of the Aberdeen University's annual theatrical production, when the audience was composed entirely of students. A riotous section of the crowd, carrying hockey sticks and other weapons heckled the poor actors mercilessly and scattered pease meal from the "gods" over the red plush seats and carpets. They invaded the bar and smashed all the glasses. The orgy of destruction was indescribable and was ended only by the arrival of the police. Next day the student representatives made abject apologies, but my father put a ban on student nights and it was many years before permission was again granted.

The 'giants' of the theatrical profession came to Aberdeen in his time and I was reminded of their names when I consulted the bound folios of programmes presented to Aberdeen Public Library by the late amateur actor A.M. Shinnie. Henry Lytton starred in all the D'Oyly Carte Opera Company's productions of Gilbert and Sullivan. Sir John Martin-Harvey played Sydney Carton in *The Only Way,* the dramatised version of Charles Dickens' story *A Tale of Two Cities.* Martin Harvey's wife Nina de Silva always played the part of Mimi in the play, and on a return visit many years later my sister and I (who were keen theatre-goers!) baked her a cake with the name Mimi in sugar icing on top.

Other famous actors and actresses who came to His Majesty's Theatre were Sir Frank Benson, H.B. Irving, Fred Terry and Julia Neilson in Sweet Nell of Old Drury, Matheson Lang, Oscar Asche and Lily Brayton in Othello, Marie Studholme, Mr and Mrs Kendal, Joseph O'Mara, Forbes Robertson, Seymour Hicks, Owen Nares, and Fay Compton in her unforgettable performance in the name part of Barrie's *Mary Rose.* His Majesty's was so well known and so popular with the profession that it was a compara-tively simple matter to fill a year's booking in advance with stars of this stature.

Looking through these old programmes which cost two (old) pennies I was struck by some of the advertisements in March 1907.

Wisharts of Rose Street offer Two Rooms Furnished Comfortably for £18.11.3.
Bon Accord Hotel — lunch or mixed grill — 1/6.
Tobacco 6d an ounce.
China Tea 2/- a lb.
Whisky 2/6 a bottle.

The programmes also intimated, "Special tram cars are arranged to wait at the theatre every evening for the Circular Route via Rosemount. Ladies' Bonnets *not* allowed in Orchestra Stalls or first three rows of Dress Circle."

In 1956 the B.B.C. broadcast a radio programme on the 50th Anniversary of the Theatre and my mother returned to Aberdeen from Oxfordshire where she was living in order to take part.

One of her earliest recollections was of a happening — I believe in September 1907 — during the production of Hall Caine's great religious play *The Christian.* On the first night my father saw that one of the leading actors was so intoxicated that he could hardly speak. His immediate suspension was ordered and the understudy took over. The actor and some of his pals in the company vowed vengeance and at the end of the show lay in wait for my father in Lower Skene Street at the back of the theatre. In those days there was no lighting and this shabby street opposite Blacks Buildings was an area of particular danger. This possibility was foreseen by young Mr Kinney, my father's secretary, who insisted on accompanying him up the street. As expected my father was attacked. As Kinney warded off the blows my father blew a long penetrating blast on the police whistle which he always carried on his key-ring. This whistle had been for long the subject of good-humoured jokes among his friends, but it stood him in good stead that night. His assailants vanished into the darkness. This whistle is in my writing desk!

Not long afterwards my father had installed an electric light over the stage door, not because of this incident but in order to scare off the "Stage-door Johnnies." They used to hang about to catch a glimpse of the attractive leading ladies in the George Edwardes Musical Comedies — *Gipsy Love, The Dollar Princess, The Merry Widow.*

The year 1918, was the year of the Armistice of the 1st World War and C.H. Webster, a critic at that time for the old newspaper *The Bon Accord*, recounted in the Jubilee broadcast what he considered the biggest night he'd ever seen at His Majesty's. The O'Mara Opera Co. were presenting a season of operas and on the night of November 11th the opera was Gounod's *Faust*. The signing of the Armistice had been announced at 11 o'clock in the morning and everyone had thronged the streets, cheering and laughing. At night the theatre was packed. When it came to the Soldiers' Chorus Joseph O'Mara himself led the soldiers onto the stage, carrying a Union Jack in each hand! He was followed by all the principals — whether in the opera or not — marching round the stage, waving banners and the flags of the Allies and singing the rousing Soldiers' Chorus.

C.H. Webster also remembered the "Littlest" night when he was the only person sitting in solitary state in the centre of the stalls. The play had been written by a suffragette and the suffragettes weren't very popular in Aberdeen. Regular playgoers expressed their disapproval by staying away!

I made my theatrical début at His Majesty's which turned out to be nearly my theatrical demise! I was very young and was cast in an amateur production presented in aid of the Red Cross by Madame Isabel Murray, well-known locally for her School of Dancing. My part was that of the little mortal girl who was looking for fairies at the bottom of the garden. Now in addition to the "Watteau" curtain, a Safety Curtain was required by law to be lowered once every performance. This, in case of fire, separates audience from stage and the regulation still obtains. Unknown to me, on the very morning of the day I was to appear, a new heavy plain grey safety curtain was installed and tested. A theatre cleaner had left her galvanised pail on the stage directly in the path of the curtain which, when it descended, squashed the pail absolutely flat. Well that night at the end of my scene, I came down to the footlights, curled up in the grass and "fell asleep". But I came down too far and lay immediately below the slowly falling safety curtain. Luckily for me, my father was in the wings and had seen what had happened to the cleaner's pail in the morning. I remember I lay there thinking, "Why doesn't the curtain come down?" I heard my father's voice, "Hold the curtain". It stopped two feet above me. Then right in front of the audience Madame Murray rushed on to the stage and much to my chagrin, dragged me backwards.

Then the curtain completed its descent. A memorable first appearance!

I said that my father was a popular figure. Several times — out of the blue — presentations were made to him by groups of friends and staff to demonstrate their affection. After ten years as manager of the theatre he was entertained at dinner by a company which included representatives of the Church, the University and Town Council and presented with a handsome oak bookcase and cabinet with beautiful 13-pane astragal glass doors. At the same time my mother was given a gold wristlet watch and necklace of pearls.

The engraved brass plate on the front of the bookcase read:

PRESENTED TO
H. ADAIR NELSON
MANAGER, HIS MAJESTY'S THEATRE
By a few friends in token of their respect and esteem
ABERDEEN 12th DECEMBER 1917

As a special treat I was occasionally permitted to go through the pass door up the narrow stairs to my father's private office, going first through the ante-room occupied by his book-keeper. There was usually a coal fire burning brightly. A large roll-top desk almost filled one wall with his swivel chair in which I used to play, revolving round and round.

Everything seemed so secure and permanent. But suddenly in 1923 the world — at least our world — changed. Robert Arthur, by then associated with Howard and Wyndham, decided to sell the theatre. It was taken over by Walter Gilbert who wished, quite naturally, to install his son Lothian Gilbert as manager. On the 3rd March of that year the liability of Robert Arthur Theatres Company ceased and the cold memorandum from the Chartered Accountants requested that the Entertainment Tax Bond be negotiated anew with Mr Gilbert; an inventory of carpets and furnishings be checked by J. & A. Ogilvie, Aberdeen and the Bar Stock of liquors, glass, chocolates and cigarettes be taken by Chivas Bros.

It all sounded so simple but it was the end of an era. My father left his beloved theatre which was his life. He took over the Management of the Palace Theatre in Bridge Place, and a few years later left for Edinburgh to become manager of the Lyceum Theatre. But he was taken ill in Edinburgh, returned home and died in April 1929.

The theatre has gone through many vicissitudes since then.
With the advent of talkies and radio the live theatre had fallen into
the doldrums and indeed the very future of what was known as the
most beautiful theatre in Great Britain was in the balance. Happily
in 1933 it was purchased by Aberdeen businessman James F.
Donald who gave it a new and vigorous lease of life.

I left Aberdeen about that time for the bright lights of a stage
career in London and am not qualified to speak from personal
experience of the great success of the Donald family — James R.
Donald and Peter Donald sons of the original J.F. Donald — in
the running of the theatre.

On the death in 1971 of James R. Donald (always known as
Jimmy Donald) his sons James F. Donald, the second, took over
as director and Peter as manager. It remained the last privately
owned theatre in Scotland until 1974 when it was bought by
Aberdeen District Council for £350,000 with the help of a grant of
£100,000 from the Scottish Arts Council. The Donalds remained
at the helm.

Two years ago it was discovered that the theatre must close for a
period of at least nine months for extensive technical modernisa-
tion. The renovation was inspired by the Health and Safety at
Work Act of 1978 which stated that hoists or lifts must be totally
enclosed in a lift shaft. The scenery hoist at His Majesty's Theatre
had open sides. To enclose and increase the size of the lift led to
countless further alterations — including a stronger bridge over
the culvert of the Denburn which flows underneath the theatre.
The saga of the restoration is too complicated to detail here. The
Council agreed that an extensive programme of restoration should
be undertaken at a cost of around £3,000,000 over a period of two
years. As the theatre is a Category A listed building its original
character will be preserved, assured by the talents of the City
Architect Ian A. Ferguson who has all over responsibilty for
design and construction.

Edi Swan, energetic technical and artistic director of the
theatre, supervises the renovation. He says his job is "to ensure
that His Majesty's will function as a theatre after all the workmen
have left."

A few months ago he invited me to join a party including James
Donald and members of the Press to visit the theatre half-way
through its restoration. Wearing red safety helmets as protection
against falling plaster we walked across the main auditorium

empty now for the red plush seats had been removed for re-upholstering. The orchestra pit was dismantled. It was cold, dark and very, very dirty. Only the contractors' lamps shone on the scaffolding. The once brilliant central chandelier lay on the floor of the stalls in a terrible state. In the flies the original brake for the Safety Curtain lay in the corner (which once saved my life?). My father's office — his desk gone, the fireplace blocked up but his swivel chair still there. The echo of hammers, planks of wood being thrown, the clank of metal on metal, sparks from the welding. The Watteau curtain cracked and discarded.

Oh there were ghosts — my father standing on his captain's bridge, the crowds chatting at the elegant dress-circle bar, Mr Rogers conducting *God Save the King*.

Much has been written about His Majesty's Theatre during the last few years — its past, its present, its future but it now attains a splendour hitherto undreamed of.

The interior colour scheme is today of pale cream and white with soft grey panels graded from dark in the roof to a soft pastel grey in the stalls. The frieze is in white and gold leaf with pale blue behind. This blue is repeated in the alcoves behind the statues and in the foyer ceiling. The blue is to balance the large area of crimson in the drapes, seats, carpet and wallpaper. Throughout, the 22 carat gold leaf brings the whole scheme alive.

It has just been announced that the Re-opening Night of His Majesty's Theatre is Friday, 17th September 1982 to be attended by the Prince of Wales. The Royal Gala Performance will have the appropriate title of *Curtain Up* and will be a lavish musical revue with dancing by the Scottish Ballet Company. There may still be some who will be able to compare it with the original Opening Performance of the operatic pantomime *Little Red Riding Hood* in December 1906!

Once more we quote the words from 'The Playhouse of Bon Accord', "Now it remains with the people of Aberdeen to put the copestone of success on what the craftsmen of Aberdeen have builded with so much care."

Acknowledgements

To the following organisations and individuals for their permission to reproduce photographs in this book.

Captain Hay of Hayfield 1.

James Kerr 6.

John G. Weir 2, and the Letters from the Crimea.

Jock Esson 9.

The Arbroath Herald 5, 8, 9, 10, 11, 12, 13, 17, 18, 19, 24, 43.

Aberdeen Journals 14, 25, 29, 32, 36.

Mrs Violet Humphrey 15, 16.

Homes and Gardens 21, 22.

The National Trust for Scotland 23 (with the kind permission of H.M. The Queen Mother) 33.

The Hunter family 26, 27.

Mary McMurtrie 28.

The BBC 31.

The Scottish Daily Record 37.

Harold Esslemont 40.

The National Gallery of Scotland, Edinburgh, 45.

Further photographs supplied by the author.

Some of the material in these chapters has previously appeared in articles written by the author in

The Arbroath Herald — Royal Gardener, Jock and Mary Esson, Invercauld and the Regalia, James Craig, His Majesty's Theatre.

The Scots Magazine — The Black Sheep of Dinnet.

The Leopard Magazine — Cocky Hunter, Jessie Kesson, People Who Have Gardens, Harold Esslemont, His Majesty's Theatre.

The Preface quoted on page 48 is re-printed from *The Golden Bridge of Memoirs* by Colonel James McGivern Humphrey, MC, © Nelson Canada 1979. Used by permission of the Publisher and Mrs Violet Humphrey.